WINNING REPUTATIONS

HOW TO BE YOUR OWN SPIN DOCTOR

by

Chris Genasi

palgrave

First published 2002 by
PALGRAVE
Houndmills, Basingstoke, Hampshire RG21 6XS and
175 Fifth Avenue, New York, N.Y. 10010
Companies and representatives throughout the world

PALGRAVE is the new global academic imprint of
St. Martin's Press LLC Scholarly and Reference Division and
Palgrave Publishers Ltd (formerly Macmillan Press Ltd).

ISBN 0–333–96365–2 paperback

This book is printed on paper suitable for recycling and
made from fully managed and sustained forest sources.

A catalogue record for this book is available
from the British Library.

Library of Congress Cataloging-in-Publication Data
has been applied for

Editing and origination by
Aardvark Editorial, Mendham, Suffolk

10 9   8   7   6   5   4   3   2   1
11 10 09 08 07 06 05 04 03 02

Printed and bound in Great Britain by
Creative Print & Design (Wales), Ebbw Vale

To Jill

Contents

List of figures ix

List of tables x

Foreword xi

Acknowledgements xiii

Chapter 1   **A good reputation is worth fighting for** 1
Rocket-fuelled reputation drivers 3
The rights and responsibilities of reputation builders 7

Chapter 2   **Mastering your reputation: the first small steps** 19

Chapter 3   **Reputation as the new religion: the powers behind
the movement** 29
Beginning the journey to a winning reputation 29
Whose reputation is it anyway? 31

Chapter 4   **Your reputation architecture: a blueprint for
a winning reputation** 51
Engineering a healthy PR genome 52
Five key stages of the reputation architecture blueprint 53
Stage 1: surveying the terrain 54
Stage 2: sketching the finished building 56
Stage 3: safe foundations 69
Stage 4: structural strength 76
Stage 5: ongoing maintenance 83

Chapter 5   **You are your PR: living out your reputation** 86
Becoming a micro celebrity 89
Working out your key messages 90
Assembling a message delivery kit for a winning reputation 96
A personal winning reputation plan you can stick to 100

Chapter 6   **Reputation as performance art** 104
Working backwards to reputation 105
Sound bites – speaking in headlines 105
Reach out when you speak out 106
Top props 108

Surprise others by surprising yourself   110
The grand gesture   111
Symbols   112

Chapter 7   **What the reputation consultants say … and
                 don't say**   **113**
                 Getting best value from PR consultants   116
                 When to turn within and when to turn without 118
                 Extracting the most from your dream consultant 120
                 The consultants' advice on consultants   122
                 What makes a great PR guru?   125

Chapter 8   **The new e-economy: what it means for those
                 building a winning reputation**   **128**
                 Internet-nots   130
                 Media meltdown   132
                 Your online information service   134
                 Making the trip worthwhile   137
                 Sales/lead generation   138
                 Internal communications   138
                 Opinion former/stakeholder communications 139
                 Content, content, content   139
                 Visual connections   140
                 Online issues and crisis management   141
                 Chat room etiquette   145
                 The dark side of the boom   146
                 The new frontier with the old rules – getting started 146

Chapter 9   **Spreading your gospel: how to turn your
                 employees into your biggest fans**   **148**
                 Three steps to turning your employees into evangelists 150
                 The symbiotic relationship between PR and HR 151
                 Creating an employee communications campaign 153
                 Workers of the world unite … into market segments 155
                 Blurred visions and missions   155
                 Putting on a show for the troops   157

Chapter 10   **Winning reputation case studies: learning from
                 the best**   **160**

Recommended further reading   192

Index   193

List of figures

3.1   Converging stakeholder interests   33
3.2   Consumers becoming corporate – results of research in France   40
3.3   Consumers becoming corporate – results of research in Germany   41
3.4   Consumers becoming corporate – results of research in Australia   42
3.5   Consumers becoming corporate – results of research in Singapore   43
3.6   Consumers becoming corporate – results of research in the USA   44

4.1   The PR genome   53
4.2   Attributes and drivers of reputation   60
4.3   The reputation ladder   68
4.4   Joined up reputation flow   77
4.5   The audience/activity checker   78
4.6   Joined up PR   79

5.1   Message mapping: master messages and trident messages   92
5.2   Message mapping: master messages, trident messages and killer facts 93
5.3   Message mapping flow chart   95

List of tables

3.1	Who matters to your business?	37
3.2	How stakeholders are converging	45
4.1	Five stages of the reputation architecture blueprint	54
4.2	*Fortune*, the *Financial Times* and *Management Today* corporate reputation criteria	58
4.3	Reputation scorecard – example	61
4.4	Criteria for judging companies	62
4.5	Reputation scorecard with stretch goals	63
4.6	Typical PR work plan	80
4.7	The five stages of the reputation architecture blueprint	85
5.1	PR action plan for Mytown	102
7.1	The consultants' view: what makes a good client?	123
7.2	What makes a great PR guru?	126

Foreword

There is only one thing in the world worse than being talked about, and that is not being talked about. (*The Picture of Dorian Gray*, Oscar Wilde, 1890)

There is a perception that the management of reputation is a new phenomenon, that it is only in today's media-filled world that highly paid image consultants and faceless government press secretaries work their sinister magic to manipulate a public, whose every mood and whim is tracked by focus groups, pollsters and psychologists.

In fact, the whole business of spin doctoring and manipulating perception is perhaps the world's second oldest profession. As the quotation above from 1890 clearly shows, caring about what people think of you is nothing new. It is a fundamental human trait and people have been managing their reputation since history began.

After all, social acceptance is one of the essential human desires expressed in Maslow's hierarchy of needs, after food and water, shelter and a mate. Being well thought of, having a good name and being admired are all important in societies across the world, and always have been and probably always will be.

The difference today is that what is a natural desire to be well considered has now been developed into a management process called public relations or reputation management. For the past 15 years or so I have been advising companies and individuals on how to use the techniques of reputation management in order to build the success of their businesses and their own personal careers.

The benefits of having a winning reputation can be secured by any organization or individual that chooses to apply him or herself to improving their profile. In this book, I will set out my suggestions on how to build a reputation that will transform your fortunes and those of your business. I will take you through the key steps towards achieving a winning reputation, based on my experience of working with multinational businesses and major organizations over the years.

It is a journey open to anyone regardless of profession or scale of the organization. While having a winning reputation does involve some particular skills which we will cover in detail in Chapters 3, 4 and 5, it is really about a state of mind and a determination to stand out from the crowd in a way that promotes your accomplishments while at the same time building a reputation magnet that attracts even more success.

CHRIS GENASI

Acknowledgements

I would like to thank the following people who have helped in the writing of this book: Sarah Hagan and Michael Guiney for assistance with the research, Peggie Wood and Linda Ruggiero for help with the graphics, Stephen Rutt and everyone at Palgrave Publishers Ltd, Philip Dewhurst at Weber Shandwick for giving me the time to write it, Dawn James also at Weber Shandwick, Phil Riggins of SWR Research for exploring new territories in reputation management, Richard Houghton of Carrot Communications, Caroline Sami of Perfect Pitch, Joanne Milroy at Weber Shandwick for the original idea, Christine Drury at Unilever, John Ballington at Lever Fabergé and Paul Atkinson at Royal & SunAlliance for road-testing some of my ideas, Charles Fombrun at New York University's Stern Business School, and Scott Meyer and Gary Thompson for encouragement, inspiration and an American perspective. Thanks are also due to all the PR consultants and members of the PR industry who supplied case studies and helped with the research: Chris McDowall (PRCA), Adrian Wheeler (GCI UK), Paul Vousden (VLP), Charles Cook (Grandfield), Stephen Byfield (PPS), Richard Allen (AD Communications Ltd), Michael Regester (Regester Larkin), Bill Nichols (The White Oaks Consultancy Ltd), Julia Willoughy (Willoughy PR), Angela Casey (Countrywide Porter Novelli), Guy Woodcock (Montpellier Marketing Communication Group), Graham Lancaster (Biss Lancaster plc), Clare Meikle (The Communication Group Scotland), Linda Taylor (JBP Associates Ltd), Julien Speed (Starfish Communications), Michael Frohlich (Shine Communications), Patrick Orr (Raitt Orr & Associates Ltd), Keith S Webb (Edson Evers & Associates Ltd), Paul Carroll (Communique PR), Tari Hibbit (Edleman PR Worldwide), Hilary Meacham (Focus PR Ltd), Christine Mortimer (PPR), Tricia Topping (TTA PR), Allan Biggar (Burson-Marsteller), Richard Price (The EuroPR Group), Nick Hindle (Phipps PR), Linda Batt-Rawden (The Impact Agency), Brian MacLaurin (MacLaurin), Graham Paskett (Paskett PR Ltd), Elizabeth Hindmarch (Elizabeth Hindmarch PR), and The IPRA for supplying many of the original case studies. Thanks to all the celebrities and sportspeople for their words of advice and finally to Jill, Grace and Louis for putting up with my absence from family life over the past few months.

CHAPTER 1

A good reputation is worth fighting for

While having a strong reputation is a choice, increasingly it is not an option if you want to stay ahead of your competitors. Just about every organization in the commercial, state and voluntary sectors has woken up to this need and as a result we are in the middle of a reputation revolution.

There is no doubt that PR and reputation management are growing dramatically in terms of investment and importance. Yet it is perhaps surprising that we are increasingly sensitive to the views of others, given the rise of the 'me culture'. It could well be imagined that the rise in individualism in many Western societies would challenge the importance of winning acknowledgement and respect within society, as people increasingly trade public and mass social acceptance for greater personal expression and individuality.

It is undoubtedly true that today we are less willing to do things or live in a certain way simply because society demands it or to keep up appearances. However, rather than diminish the need to be well thought of in society, the impact on how reputations are managed has been more subtle and complex. The rise of individualism has not in fact destroyed the basic human wish to be respected and admired by one's peers.

The difference is that a more individualistic society has created more demand for the professional management of reputation as audiences have fragmented. Today there are several discrete peer groups and target audiences where one seeks approval and acceptance, as opposed to a homogeneous population holding a single set of values shared, by and large, by the whole of society, as in the past. As society splinters, so does the need to manage one's reputation in a systematic way with the specific audience groups that count.

Today's companies, governments, organizations and individuals no longer think about their public as a single entity. Instead of 'the public', people talk about 'publics' or stakeholders. These are overlapping groups of people, each requiring a slightly different, tailored approach if we want to seek their opinion, influence or win them over.

The fragmentation of the media and society in general makes this specific targeting of a series of audiences – as opposed to mass audience communication – a prerequisite for those looking to keep on top of how they are perceived. Caring about what others think of us is still a strong driver for humans, the only difference is that this is becoming more and more complex as a one-message-fits-all approach proves increasingly ineffective.

We all know instinctively that having a good reputation is important. Not just because most of us prefer to be liked and respected, but having a good reputation is often also essential in terms of financial and social success. A good reputation is a competitive edge worth acquiring. It can help you to get a job, and people will come to you with ideas and suggestions which can open up opportunities. A good reputation can help you to gain goodwill credits, which build up in your goodwill bank account and eventually buy you the reputational equivalent of the freedom of the city.

In all sorts of situations you will be given the benefit of the doubt, a sporting chance and a free rein, all because of the one factor that a good reputation bestows: trust. Trust is the dividend of investing in your reputation. It is trust that persuades people to open their doors to you. Trust will win over voters, consumers, co-workers, employers, employees, investors, opponents – whomever you wish to influence.

A strong reputation helps to enhance what is already there. It is like an invisible lens magnifying assets to create an illusion of scale, substance and capability. Reputation causes someone to spring to mind when thinking of the way forward and convinces us that that person is capable of taking on new challenges and can be trusted.

Reputation makes us feel comfortable with people and things, it attracts, reassures and inspires us to put our faith and often our hard earned cash into supporting a person, product, business or cause.

Without the reassurance of reputation, everyday decisions around which products to buy, who to employ, which shares to invest in, which clothes to buy, even where to live or go on holiday would all be decisions made in the dark. Reputation provides a touchstone in a world full of unknowns. It helps us to find the wheat among the chaff.

While reputation has always been vital, there can be no doubt that its importance has grown dramatically over the past 20 years. The change has been building rapidly and has become, for anyone in public or commercial life, totally unavoidable.

To begin to understand how to manage one's profile and build a winning reputation, it is useful to understand the drivers behind our modern-day obsession with the age-old desire to manage perception.

Rocket-fuelled reputation drivers

There have been five main drivers of change over the past 20 years which have seen the stellar rise in importance of reputation management as a key part of successful political or commercial life. They are:

- the death of deference

- more and more media

- me first and foremost

- fast news

- money makes the reputation go round

and we will now examine each driver in turn.

The death of deference

In the past, people simply accepted what they were told by those who controlled society. Generally religious leaders, monarchs, community chiefs, even family elders were not questioned. Their social position was their reputation, and their standing was guaranteed regardless of their abilities or credibility.

Because of this unquestioned authority, opinion formers and decision makers (generally speaking) had to worry less about winning over public support once they had attained their position of power. Clearly this is no longer the case. The rise of democracy and the rights of the individual have led to a society where people are far less accepting of the actions and views of those in power, either politically, commercially or socially.

People today are increasingly sceptical, require proof, will challenge and probe in a way that was unheard of in previous centuries or even decades. The public no longer accept things at face value; they no longer assume that because of a person's position or status that individual, or the organization he or she represents, must be unconditionally believed or their opinions automatically accepted.

This presents new challenges for those who are required to communicate with the public and other audiences. Your word is not enough on its own. You need to be highly credible, capable of scrutiny and cross-examination. You will need to demonstrate that you are listening and responsive and, above all, you need to be seen to be trustworthy. This is no longer a right of birth or position, today this trust must be earned and maintained.

More and more media

The second key change in the reputation landscape is the growth and fragmentation of the media. Not only has the media changed to reflect the sceptical, challenging style of its readers, but it has also grown in scale and breadth to reflect the insatiable desire for information and editorial guidance in a complex world. A world where we demand and need to find out things for ourselves, such as what to buy, where to go on holiday, who to vote for, what savings plan to take out, which car to buy, which restaurant to eat in, what sort of marriage to have, or how to bring up our children.

We need the media to be our trusted editorial guide to the world. We need to locate reliable journalists who can help us to sieve through the official corporate babble, glossy brochures and slick advertising to determine what is really going on.

The less we accept things at face value, the more we need to investigate for ourselves. But this takes effort and we need the media to help us to save time and reach the best conclusions for us as individuals. People have always looked to trusted individuals in a society to help to editorialize the world, sorting out the hype from the hip, the vacuous from the valuable. We simply do not have the time to find things out for ourselves. We all need to lean on people who can deliver trusted independent advice to help us to make informed decisions, free – or so we think – of the manipulation of vested interests.

The modern media also helps to keep those in positions of power on their toes, asking those awkward questions on our behalf. It stands up for us. The media understands our world, our values and our needs and acts like a big brother, standing up to potential bullies in the playground, protecting us, ensuring fair play and good treatment.

This expanded campaigning role of the media has led also to an explosion in the quantity and specificity of the media. There are now hundreds of thousands of publications both in print and on the Web. Every special interest is catered for, every age group, ethnic group, social type and lifestyle tribe is covered. There are magazines that campaign on specific issues such as the environment, those that champion personal rights and self-fulfilment, those that help people to make purchasing decisions on cars, boats, cameras and so on. The list is vast and reflects the growing awareness and need for the media to be not only broad in its appeal, but also to appeal to very specific groups or cover particular areas in great detail.

This fragmentation and multiplication in the breadth and quantity of the media brings massive challenges for those managing reputation. The demands of the media are insatiable. It is quite normal in a major corporation for a press office of, say, four or five people to be fully occupied 7 days per week, 52 weeks per year, doing nothing other than responding to the demands and requests of journalists. And the media expects this level of service. When it asks a question, it expects an answer. When it wants information, it anticipates getting it – for free.

'No comment' is not possible. Refusing to comment to the media is a response route that is hardly ever followed now. To say 'No comment' would now be seen as bizarre. Today, we all have to comply with media scrutiny if we want to be part of society.

Me first and foremost

Another key factor in the rise in the importance of reputation is the importance of the individual in society. Today we expect more for ourselves. Our views count. We believe that we should not do what we are told, we should tell what is to be done. The individual increasingly drives commercial and political agendas, not the other way around. The dependence on market research as the subsoil on which the foundations of decision making are laid is now established in every walk of life.

While market research has for some time been commonplace in commercial companies, it is now central to political policy making, and even traditionally nonconsumer-led organizations such as the Church or state departments are increasingly listening to the views and demands of people, in order to help them to develop new ways of maintaining relevance to the public and ensure their ongoing support.

Those organizations that want people to behave in certain ways and believe in certain things must first of all learn to listen to what people are saying, if nothing else to check whether anyone might be interested in their point of view, let alone whether they might accept it. Leading business and political figures are now often in the totally new position of having those they seek to influence telling them what it is they are willing to be influenced about.

In such a topsy-turvy, complex arrangement, the peace treaty between the individual and those in authority is trust. Trust is what will get people at least listening and the growth of trust will flourish with the fertilizer of a strong reputation.

Fast news

The speed of global communications is another significant factor that has boosted the importance of reputation. The reason is simply that there is no hiding place for reputation skeletons. You have to bring out your dead even if you do not want to. Global, high speed communications will spread bad news like an epidemic. Inconsistencies between countries or audience groups are thrown into sharp relief by the instantaneous comparisons drawn by global media. We see environmental groups and unions use global media to fan the flames of a debate, as like-minded individuals world-wide are mobilized to support what might otherwise have been a local matter.

Awareness built through the global media of what is happening in similar situations elsewhere in the world can accelerate change at home. For example, if we learn that in other countries they pay lower taxes on certain items or that people doing the same job are paid more by the same company, we feel more confident and justified to ask for these changes in our own market. In turn, it makes it harder for companies, politicians and others in power to attempt to resist this change, if a precedent elsewhere in the world has been highlighted by the global media.

Reputation managers now swim in a global fish bowl. Anything they do in one place will be seen everywhere else and almost instantaneously. Managing this dimension of growing globalization in the media in terms of reputation building requires resources, expertise and an attitude that recognizes that all life is public and requires reputation to be managed actively, as an asset, and traded on the electronic global media stock exchange.

Money makes the reputation go round

Growing wealth and disposable income is the fifth factor that has driven the importance of reputation. Of course, as people have greater amounts of disposable income they are able to buy more. However, more significantly, they are able to be more discerning, electing to purchase brands that deliver on price and quality, but which also provide emotional attributes. Increasingly, consumers expect the companies behind brands to live by a set of values of which they approve. The days of brands being commodities, where consumer choice was based on the simplest of factors, have been replaced by a more complex set of socially responsible requirements that need to be met before brands become acceptable.

Today more and more consumers can afford to buy shares and take out personal pensions and savings schemes based on the performance of the stock market. In choosing these, reputation becomes a critical factor in creating differentiation.

While it is true that consumers have more to spend, businesses need to work harder to win their trust in order that they accept their branded promises. Wealth offers consumers a choice and creates a sophistication of the market which moves consumer purchases from subsistence-based choices to decisions that require guilt-free enjoyment and fulfilment. How can a consumer feel comfortable in a shirt if he or she knows that it was stitched by children earning a fraction of the purchase price? The consumer looks to business to deal with this feeling of guilt on their behalf.

The rights and responsibilities of reputation builders

Clearly the commercial world must rise to the challenge of building the confidence and trust demanded by consumers across the globe. But while it is clear that reputation is more important today than ever, what still remains a mystery is why so many people in positions of authority, businesses and organizations leave their reputation largely to chance.

To reiterate Oscar Wilde's opinion, not only is not being talked about worse than being talked about, it is actually damaging not to be talked about. Reputation abhors a vacuum and if you do not manage your reputation, others will. This is a key insight that so many in business and public life fail to see. Instead they assume that keeping their head down will prevent it getting chopped off. In fact keeping your head down simply means that you end up walking into things and not seeing others running away with your treasures.

Sadly, many organizations feel that it is not even worth trying to sculpt their reputation profile. Too many business leaders, managers and others for whom reputation really matters believe that their reputation is something that just happens. Or, at most, that it is something that you have and the best you can do is hold on to it without making any mistakes, or at least getting caught making any mistakes.

This is just not good enough, given the importance of reputation today. The fact is – and this is the most important message in this book and the most important piece of advice you will hear from any practitioner in the reputation business – anyone can have a winning reputation if they choose to and if they are willing to work hard at building one.

In a world where, increasingly, perception is reality, building a good reputation is no longer the act of an egoist, but rather the duty of any responsible person who is looking to manage their business in a professional, sustainable way.

Reputation development is surely one of the two key roles (along with providing cultural leadership) of any business leader. Whether it is talking up the stock price, inspiring the workforce or selling directly to customers, leadership and reputation building underpin so much of the actual success that a company enjoys.

However, it would be wrong to imply that business people are not more attuned to the importance of reputation than in the past. In over 15 years as a PR consultant, I have seen an increase in major corporations and brands using PR to help to communicate with key stakeholder groups in order to develop a strong reputation as an environment in which the business can flourish.

Indeed, the growth of the global PR consultancy market reflects the higher ranking given by businesses to the management of their reputation. Fifteen years ago in the UK, the number one PR consultancy had an annual fee income of around £5 million. Today the UK's market leader has billings of around £30 million. Reputation management and PR in general are clearly defined areas within the marketing mix and the subject is taken seriously on boardroom agendas. This has led to more attention and ever larger budgets allocated by corporations to reputation management.

However, what has been evident is that much of this growth has been driven by fear of reputation meltdown rather than an active desire to build reputation capital. The entry point for most corporations to the world of serious reputation development has been as a result of the 'there but for the grace of God' factor.

Companies witness other businesses being severely damaged or even destroyed by PR disasters and can all too easily envisage their own organization in similar straits. High profile incidents such as Bhopal, Shell's Brent Spar affair, Nike's child labour experience and the attrition of the tobacco industry have made hairs stand up on the necks of global CEOs the world over. Added to this, there has been the rise in power of activist groups and nongovernmental organizations, fuelled by a faster, more aggressive global electronic media. These three horsemen of the reputation apocalypse have swirled through the collective nightmares of multinational business leaders and spurred even the most reactionary of companies to review their crisis management plans in terms of reputation risk.

If there was a patron saint for corporate crises, PR people world-wide would gratefully carry their icons along with their Palm Pilots wherever they went and would give thanks to the boost that these catastrophic incidents have given to the PR industry. Behind every ambulance there is a lawyer and behind them a PR person.

But this is not just ruthless exploitation. There is no doubt that, under the cold light of the media's microscope and the uncompromising probes of pressure groups, politicians and regulators, companies have become more aware of their responsibilities to society and have kick-started corporate re-engineering programmes which have seen genuine improvements in corporate citizenship. Often PR people are the catalysts for these corporate atonement initiatives.

It may be true that the motive was originally fear of being caught in a reputation black spot. However, companies have understood quickly that this is not just useful in terms of avoiding trouble, but it can also help to improve the standing of the business in the eyes of employees, investors, customers, local communities and other stakeholder groups. In short, attempts to improve the behaviour of the business have led to all manner of unexpected benefits. Indeed, it seems that a good reputation is good for the bottom line as well as the soul.

For example, as a result of criticism of its involvement in Nigeria and other countries, Shell has introduced new, clear guidelines for global staff on doing business around the world, leading to a more transparent and consistent way of operating. Many major multinationals now have firm guidelines on ethical issues, such as policies on bribery and corporate gifts, use of child labour, sensitivity to local cultures and social responsibility to communities, areas above and beyond their responsibility in law.

Companies surely know that thorough preparation for reputation issues and the systematic development of crisis and issues management plans for their businesses are essential insurance measures that every organization should take. At long last, protection of reputation is a real priority for every business that is serious about its responsibilities, even if that sense of responsibility extends to shareholders alone.

However, even this limited view of those stakeholders that matter is changing. Most businesses are now aware of the importance of audiences other than shareholders. Indeed, professional reputation management with all stakeholders is a key part in delivering the shareholder value that is so often the raison d'être cited by many CEOs for their business.

Yet, while reputation protection is now fairly standard practice, reputation promotion is still a largely untapped source of competitive edge. This is a missed opportunity that can be likened to putting only an undercoat of paint on a house rather than finishing the job to perfection.

The aim of reputation protection (the vast majority of effort in this field) is really a neutral outcome. No bad publicity is the goal. Radio silence, anonymity and conformity are the key performance indicators for those who limit themselves to reputation protection. It is the equivalent of ensuring that you have a healthy body, but never actually using that body to enjoy life.

What so many companies and business people fail to do is go to the next level and actually look to build a reputation that will be useful to the business, help to drive growth, address issues and solve the problems faced by the business and the people running it.

Why business people choose not to have a great reputation – when it is within their gift to do so – is something that baffles PR practitioners every day of the week. Opportunities to be profiled in the media, speak at high profile conferences, stand out from the competition through creative use of the media are regularly turned down by the very business people who are paying their PR teams to seek these opportunities in the first place.

Many businesses have reputational ambitions above their confidence and ability level. In today's business world it is fine to have ideas above your station, the trouble is that most business people are never willing to try and improve their reputational lot in life.

Really there is very little to fear. Building a strong reputation for yourself or your business and its products is an option open to everyone. The door policy is free and easy: if you are interesting, you can come in. A good name can be created relatively easily. All it takes is some application, observation, and effort.

The irony is that having a good reputation does not depend to any great extent on being significantly better than your competitors or colleagues. Those that believe that a good reputation will occur naturally for those people who simply do a good job are missing significant opportunities.

In reality, many talented people or good companies are overlooked or never really achieve as much as they could, not because they are in any way inferior, but simply because they are less well known. Genuinely talented people, brands and companies have the reputations they deserve; whether that reputation is strong or weak, however, depends less on the quality of their work and more on the persistence and priority they give to self-promotion.

The goal of anyone taking their public persona seriously is to achieve a reputation that they do not deserve; in other words, to have a higher profile than the sheer size or quality of your business or your personal experience would achieve without the support of any promotional activity.

Smaller, less accomplished competitors frequently achieve a far greater share of the limelight than they deserve thanks to clever management of their image. There is no doubt that reputation can give you an unfair competitive edge. In many cases, the successful way that a company promotes itself, or the manner in which an individual business person has built a high profile, means that they have a standing which is superior even though they are not actually any better at what they do than their competitors. Many excellent companies and individuals are often misunderstood or are simply unsung heroes; however, in business, wallflowers end up going to the wall.

Perception does not replace reality, but perception certainly can enhance reality. It is important to stress at this point that good image management is absolutely not a substitute for a lack of reality. The notion that PR is a magic wand that can spin a story, create good news where none exists, and transform base metal into gold is totally unfounded. You cannot have a virtual reputation any more than you can make virtual profits.

Even the best image makers cannot make people think that a sow's ear is a silk purse. However, they can educate swine to appreciate pearls. The mistake that many people make when they decide to adopt a more active approach to managing their reputation is that they see PR as a faster and cheaper alternative to genuine change. Wrong. They believe that PR will act as a smokescreen to divert critical audiences from the real issues of the day. Wrong again. They hope that PR will become another tool for evasion of genuine improvement and progress. This is not only cynical and morally corrosive for everyone involved but it is actually a waste of time and money, as it will not be successful in changing perceptions and business results in any sustainable way.

It is possible to fool enough of the people all of the time, but it hardly makes you feel proud of your work and it certainly won't provide a long-term fix, eventually you will have to face up to doing your job properly.

Of course it is right that business people have to try and put their best foot forward, even if this means omitting or not stressing any negative aspects. After all, we are all in business to make profits and sometimes survival is the goal. However, all businesses must eventually focus on sustainability, whether that be of profit or staff retention or any other factor, and will soon conclude that addressing reputation at a surface level only is the beginning of the end for any company.

Early in my career as a PR consultant, one of the world's largest construction companies was my client. One day the head of the house building division found himself with a considerable amount of unwanted publicity following reports in the consumer media, which produced a stream of disgruntled house buyers – all his customers.

The media coverage presented tales of dreams shattered by dream homes. Stories flooded in from consumers who having moved into their new homes found them to be badly built and, in some cases, dangerous. Leaking roofs, windows that did not close, windows that did not open, cracked walls, faulty plumbing, dubious electrics and flaky paintwork were just some of the problems that consumers were experiencing as they started new lives in their new homes.

The builders called in the PR team and I remember a very flustered company director saying 'I need you to stop this negative PR – what do you suggest?' Having investigated the complaints and talked to our clients about the facts behind the media stories, our advice was straightforward: 'If you want better PR, you need to build better houses.'

This tale had a happy ending for the home builder, its customers and us as PR advisers. Following this incident the company introduced a new build-quality scheme which did improve their PR, but, critically, actually improved their homes and levels of customer satisfaction.

The warning note from experiences such as this for business people and PR practitioners is that PR cannot be used as the corporate equivalent of papering over the cracks of serious business deficiencies. All too often business people look with envy at other companies and business people with outstanding reputations and assume that their stature is achieved simply through 'good PR'. The truth is far more subtle. The view that PR is capable, on its own, of building great reputations is both cynical and incorrect. I can think of only two examples where fancy PR footwork created an undeservedly favourable image. In both cases the products and services involved were adequate, but the way the media reported them was considerably more exciting and positive than was warranted.

PR had packaged these products skilfully, by tuning in to the interests, prejudices and obsessions of the media itself. The hype really did over-shadow reality. However, these are extremely rare incidents in my experience. Even the sharpest PR practitioner cannot guarantee such miracles more than once every ten years or so. If you are in the business of selling pigs' ears, it is usually better to make the best pigs' ears you can. That way you will be able to buy a silk purse in which to put all your new sales income.

PR people are not alchemists. They are more like self-improvement counsellors or personal fitness trainers. They provide plans and strategies to help their clients to attain a healthy body and a happy mind. The pursuit of physical and mental well-being requires self-awareness, analysis, review of current activity, development of a plan for change and, crucially, actually making change happen through regular visits to the gym or to therapy sessions. The same applies to the search for PR nirvana. 'Get good PR quick' schemes are as illusory as 'Get fit quick' and 'Get rich quick' schemes. Anything worth having is not easily won and this applies to PR as much as it does in other aspects of life. Many find this a disappointing revelation when the news is broken to them by their PR adviser. But the truth is that while fame is achievable overnight, reputation takes a little longer to earn. There are no short cuts. A sustainable, consistently favourable reputation requires a long-term commitment to the twin peaks of self-improvement and self-promotion. However, this should encourage rather than deter serious business people. While reputation building does require some serious application of resources for those willing to make the effort, it is an achievable goal for everyone.

Many people make the mistake of thinking that PR and reputation management are simply about obtaining coverage in the media and giving everyone a warm fuzzy feeling. This is not only lazy thinking, it denies you and your organization the full power that can be obtained from reputation management as a business problem-solving tool.

This limited view is as wide of the mark as the opinion held by those that think that PR is unnecessary if you simply do a good job. 'Do a good job and your reputation will look after itself' is the naive line of thought often heard. The truth – as is often the case – lies in the middle of the spectrum between the following two opposing views: on one extreme that PR is totally unnecessary if you are successful at what you do, and the other extreme, which concludes that clever PR can sell anything.

If all this seems too much effort, it might be worth reflecting on the wide range of things that reputation management can offer to you as an individual and to your business. A winning reputation can help to deliver results in the following areas:

Personal career development

- By securing editorial in your professional trade media featuring yourself, you will be noticed by others within your organization and your industry.

- Sturdy promotion of your ideas in the media and at conference events, for example, will position you as someone with something interesting to say in your area of expertise.

- An original point of view will help to differentiate you from the crowd and cast you in people's minds as a person with potential to take on greater responsibilities and new roles.

- A starring role in the soap opera that is your industry sector will bring you to the attention of headhunters and competitors who will be more likely to court you with improved job offers in your chosen field.

- In addition, building a profile in your industry media and elsewhere will improve your standing with your own staff as they begin to respect you for your public life as well as for what they see every day in the office.

Promotion of your business or brand to consumers

- This is perhaps the most obvious area where reputation management and PR can help you and your business. Clearly editorial endorsement of your products or company in the media will help to increase sales. First, due to simple raising of awareness and, second, due to the building of trust that is created when an independent authority, such as a journalist, recommends something. This is well illustrated in Case Study 10.24 on how Unilever's Domestos brand has built a leadership position in the area of hygiene by developing close relationships with scientific and health-related professionals and academics in the areas of hygiene and health. Similarly, Case Study 2.2 of Coca-Cola's SpriteBall campaign in Kenya is a classic example of using sports celebrities to enhance brand excitement.

- There is no established scientific analysis which proves by how much more people are influenced by editorial or other third-party endorsement than by advertising. However, any consumer research that does take place – not to mention common sense – shows that a positive review in the media from a trusted source about your company or your product will be believed far more than if you place an advertisement promoting your business.

- Third-party endorsement is tremendously powerful, whereas an advertisement is paid for by the company and the content is naturally totally controlled and biased. This does not mean that PR is more effective than advertising in changing behaviour and attitudes, simply that it has a very powerful complementary role in providing credibility to claims made in conventional, paid for communication and marketing techniques.

Attraction of investors

▪ When looking to attract investors for first or send round funding, the case will be greatly helped if the business or the idea being promulgated has achieved some media coverage or if the key management figures have a high profile through media relations and other methods of raising interest.

▪ Trust and faith in the business and the senior management behind it will be enhanced as a result, and investors are likely to be greatly reassured.

Attracting and retaining talented staff

▪ In many sectors there is a tremendous shortage of skilled labour. The best candidates are aware that they can be highly selective in a competitive market.

▪ Today's worker is looking for a lot more from a company than in the past. Training schemes, a prestigious name on the CV, a stimulating and rewarding working experience, flexible hours, pleasant offices, duvet days – the list of soft benefits seems to grow longer with every new HR fad.

▪ Employers need to use the media, trade bodies, colleges, university career teams, recruitment agencies and headhunters to create a buzz around their place of work in order to appeal to a fickle workforce which is looking for a lot more than a pay cheque.

▪ The most talented people are likely to be the most discerning and your company must stand out as a great place to work – reputation management can help to deliver this promise to the employment market.

▪ Employers need to make sure that the benefits of working at their particular company are well known and talked about so that the company becomes a destination for the best talent in its sector.

Attracting possible merger and acquisition partners

▪ Whenever a large corporation is looking around at possible acquisition targets or for possible joint partners, one of the first calls will be to ask around in the sector to find out who are the movers and shakers.

▪ Profile building articles in the media will get you noticed.

▪ Trade associations are also often consulted, so a high profile there can keep your name and that of your company uppermost when opportunity comes knocking.

Assisting dealings with suppliers

▣ Many forward thinking companies have a full communications plan in place that targets their key suppliers.

▣ The rationale is that if you let suppliers become closer in their understanding of your business goals, they can participate more fully in helping you to reach those objectives.

▣ For example, it is common for Japanese car manufacturers to have very open relationships with suppliers, where, for example, both businesses might work together to achieve cost savings which are then shared between both companies.

▣ As with all stakeholders, suppliers are more likely to feel connected to your business if they understand your broad goals and values – only then will they see their role in that plan. This can often lead to better decision making and a more creative working relationship, with suppliers seeing themselves as partners rather than traditional detached businesses, dotted along the supply chain.

Helping to support applications for planning permission or other regulatory considerations

▣ A PR campaign that promotes the benefits of a business operating in a certain area, or which highlights the contribution that that business makes to the local and national economy, will help to support appeals and proposals to regulatory authorities.

▣ Often building a positive reputation generally will be helpful if your business moves to a new area. A positive reputation precedes you like an ambassador, so that when you arrive, there is already a degree of awareness and trust created by your good name.

▣ Similarly, in legislative considerations, a well-respected and trusted company will be more likely to be invited to submit its point of view to decision makers, than will a total stranger.

Influencing the political and legislative process

▣ Professionally managed communications activity can legitimately influence the democratic process to ensure that the interests of a business or a group of individuals are not overlooked and are given due attention.

- A well-articulated reputation management programme can convey key facts which can significantly influence the outcome of new laws and political decisions.

Attracting new customers

- An established reputation will help to ensure that your company is considered as a player in your market and is frequently included in tender lists.

- Maintaining a high profile can help your business to be prominent, even when the actual size of the business might not warrant it.

- In many professions, some of the most well-known practitioners are often small players, yet their profile means they attract the best staff and customers. These companies may be small but their corporate personas are larger than life.

Facilitating brand extension or moving into new markets

- A strong reputation rubs off onto every aspect of your business, making people think that your business or brand is innovative, modern and capable of taking on new challenges. This can often mean that should you look to diversify or move into new areas, your reputation capital will underpin the move, bankrolling you with reputation credit to support your new venture.

- If your business or brand is seen as a trusted source, then your expansion plans will be more accepted and there will be a greater expectation of quality and success, despite a limited track record in this new arena.

- A good reputation is a highly elastic asset that can help you and your business to trampoline into new areas from a high ground position. An excellent example of this is shown in Case Study 10.10 of Persil, Unilever's leading detergent brand, which has successfully extended into new formats such as detergent tablets.

Addressing specific business issues, for example reducing accidents in the workplace, raising consumer loyalty and growing incremental sales

- Communication plans and PR programmes can achieve pretty much anything. Most business problems can be ameliorated or removed by improved communications that engage and mobilize people to find a solution.

▪ Clearly there needs to be substance behind the communications. But when there is, PR can be used to 'sell' virtually anything, given its strength as a discipline to explain issues, build trust and then make clear a call to action.

Just this brief glance shows the breadth of applications for PR in today's business world and the benefits it can bring. Scepticism over the importance of managing communications and reputation is disappearing quickly and more and more people are taking their reputation into their hands, shaping it, building it and benefiting from it.

This book will show you how to have an outstanding reputation. It provides a step-by-step guide to making you and your business a legend. It will show you how individuals and even the smallest businesses can learn from the multinationals and the national government publicity machines and apply modern PR and reputation management thinking to their everyday lives.

Following these simple processes will give you a winning reputation that will transform any business and develop your own personal profile and career success. The way forward is relatively easy. The only thing remaining is for you to decide that you want to have a great reputation and to take control of making that goal a reality.

CHAPTER 2

Mastering your reputation: the first small steps

Everyone has a reputation, including yourself. Think of a range of people, the famous, colleagues, people in your community, your family members, brief acquaintances and close personal friends, every one will have a reputation that exists in your mind. Each of these individuals is a unique, highly complex miracle, a bundle of emotions, feelings, experiences and features. Their lives are rich, their experiences are many.

However, you can probably sum them up – in terms of their overall reputation – in two or three sentences. Even that is possibly generous. Two or three words probably could do the job. Think of those daytime talk shows, where people have on-screen captions under their name that give a brief descriptor of who they are and why they are on the show: 'Married to husband's boss', 'Housewife turned belly dancer', 'Executive turned eco warrior', whoever we are, we can all be boiled down to a condensed four-word syrup.

It is a fact of life that people like to label others, it makes those around us easy to categorize and remember. Modern media exacerbates this. If we all have to fit in our moment of fame, there is not much time to make lengthy introductions. We live in a world where everything needs to be in bite-size chunks if you want people to swallow things.

Normally we think of this pigeonholing as a negative feature. Often it is. By reducing human beings to three-word labels, we deny the nuances and textures that go to make up the human existence. Labels encourage prejudice and lager-lout thinking. But although we know it is wrong, stereotypes are always popular as they help to make a complex and bewildering world feel a little more comfortable. It is tempting to snuggle up into well-worn ways of thinking – far easier than recognizing that there are more shades of grey than you can possibly imagine and that humans are more likely to be full of paradox rather than predictability.

However, in terms of building reputation, the human tendency to label and pigeonhole is a fact of life that should be managed to one's advantage.

Think of yourself appearing on a daytime show and consider what you would like the caption below your name to say. Or imagine the morning after a high school reunion party, when the people who had not seen you for ten years are relaying their impressions of you to others. What are the first three sentences you would like them to say about you? Alternatively, think about what a headhunter might be told about you if they called a business associate to do some investigation into your suitability for a key job.

As well as imagining what sort of things you would like them to say, also think about what they might say now, and work backwards from there to envisage a plan which will move them from saying what they think today to what you want them to think of you in the future.

Know how you *want* to be seen and how you *are* seen now and develop a clear plan on how to close this gap. That is the basis for managing your reputation. It is as simple as that.

For many in the public eye – celebrities, politicians, business leaders – this is an instinct. However, like most instincts, it is a something that can be sharpened and developed over time. At the end of this chapter, there are snippets from famous people from every walk of life. Actors, sportsmen, politicians and individuals who have achieved a prominent and positive reputation share their one piece of overall advice on achieving a good reputation.

Their words of wisdom and influential thoughts are here for you to learn from. As you read them, you will see that they fall broadly into two camps. First, there are those that feel that the best way to achieve reputation nirvana is to simply 'be yourself'. Then there is the group which takes a more planned route, and has a 'policy' or an 'approach' which they have found works for them.

The fact is that both views are correct. To build a good reputation you need to 'be yourself', but you also need a clear plan and set of tactics to ensure that 'yourself' is interesting and well communicated and understood.

Just being yourself is unlikely to deliver a strong reputation, although it is possible, it is unpredictable. Similarly, having a plan to be famous and well liked is also unlikely to succeed on its own. You need to meld these two approaches into one holistic effort.

While we can all learn by emulating successful people, even the best of us could do with a helping hand in promoting ourselves and our achievements. This is where the PR and communications experts come in and take what is already strong and make it well known. 'Truth well told' is how the global advertising agency McCann Erickson describes this process.

As well as applying to individuals, the rules of building a winning reputation apply equally to companies and institutions. Chapter 10 provides numerous case studies of organizations that have used PR to great effect. Many of them have employed it to pull themselves out of a reputational hole. Others have tapped into the creative power of public relations to ensure that they are re-appraised by their target audiences. Some have used PR to increase sales, a few to tackle complex legislative or regulatory issues and others to communicate with and engage the support of their workforces or local communities.

The range is wide and I hope that these case studies provide you with inspiration and insight. What they show time and time again is that companies can and do change their reputational fortunes. You are not stuck with your image – we can all do something about changing how we are seen and turning our reputation to our advantage – whether that be from a business point of view or a personal career perspective.

I will provide you with the building blocks of how to achieve success for yourself and your own business or organization. Over the coming chapters you will see that you can paint a winning reputation by numbers. You will realize that anyone can become a star in their particular galaxy. There is no magic (or very little) behind building a reputation. It is as planable and structured as building a set of book shelves or learning how to play a sport or a musical instrument.

All that is required is a good set of plans – which I hope to provide in this book – some role models (again, the case studies should spur you on) plus a great deal of practice and determination (these two are up to you).

To set you off and encourage you to read the rest of this book to find out how to do things for yourself, I want to present two case studies which for me epitomize the fact that a good reputation is a choice that can be exercised by anyone willing to apply their mind. These are inspirational case studies from which we can all draw confidence when everything in the reputational garden looks a little bare and wild.

After reading these, I guarantee that you will be intrigued and determined that your own reputation should become just as good, if not better. That being the case, the next chapter looks at the mindset that you need to adopt in order to be up there with the best of the reputation builders.

These are examples of good practice from the corporate world. But this book is also about how to promote your personal reputation – how to be your own spin doctor and create a winning reputation for you the brand. The lessons set out in this book are just as applicable to an individual as to a business, so everything you read here about building a winning reputation can be applied to your work as well as to your personal career progression.

The hemp launch

THE BODY SHOP, CANADA

The Body Shop of Canada's decision to introduce a controversial new line featuring hemp seed oil was launched in very effective style after the government regulator threatened it might seize the retail chain's full supply of the product.

Strategic Objectives Inc., a specialist PR firm, were brought in five weeks before the launch, in accordance with the company's policy of handling all promotion without advertising. Anita Roddick, founder of The Body Shop International, agreed to participate in the launch programme, which aimed to introduce, explain and gain credibility for hemp as a safe, effective and desirable treatment for dry skin.

The PR team also wanted to create some positive news to drive sales, manage issues and address the misinformation around hemp and to distinguish it from marijuana. Finally, there was a corporate reputation at stake as The Body Shop Canada – after the threat from the regulator – wanted to rebuild its good name.

Beyond the media kits, there was full media training to respond to journalists' questions and a launch event featuring a pro-hemp panel of speakers. However, a few days prior to the launch, Health Canada, the official state organization, warned that it might enforce a cancellation order. The response was a new plan for a nonproduct launch, named 'Maybe yes, maybe no hemp launch'. This involved blacking out signage to the event, fixing samples so that they could not be taken and providing literature with glued pages that could not be read. Two sets of speeches were prepared, one announcing a launch and one expressing regret that it was cancelled.

A new media alert was distributed to inform the media how the story had changed, and the launch was successfully repositioned as hard news. Negotiations between The Body Shop Canada and Health Canada went on, and at 6pm the night before launch, the company received permission to sell its product. This was one of the most successful launches in The Body Shop's 20-year history, with audience reach during the negotiations exceeding 11.9 million. In addition, initial sales beat all forecasts.

SpriteBall

SPRITE/COCA-COLA

Sprite, one of Coca-Cola's core beverages, was suffering from an undefined and faceless image in its 17- to 24-year-old target market in northern African countries. Audience research in Kenya established that Sprite enjoyed the image of a status badge, like Nike. The target market had few interesting leisure activities for their free time, but were avid followers of NBA basketball on television, but a lack of equipment was holding back widespread participation in the sport.

The research showed that the target audience in Kenya would welcome any initiative that developed the sport locally, but it was also clear that any programme would also need to incorporate music and other style-related activities if it was going to grab fully the attention of the target group.

The solution was the launch of SpriteBall, a competition based on the popular 3-on-3 American street basketball game. The company hoped that SpriteBall would be the vehicle through which it could generate interest in the brand and create an exciting 'cool attitude' image that resonated with the target market.

Coca-Cola decided to trial the promotion in Kenya, and set out to achieve a share of the media's sports coverage for the campaign. The PR team targeted the major schools in Kenya's eight largest towns, and the SpriteBall competition was planned to run over 10 weeks, starting at the end of term.

A SpriteBall logo was developed and basketball backboards and basketballs were purchased for distribution. Venues for the competitions were publicized and special press kits were created. Co-ordination with major regional bottlers ensured adequate supplies in the right places at the right times.

A SpriteBall demonstration team of leading basketball players was recruited to build some excitement around each event for the media and the public.

The SpriteBall contests were held over a 10-week period of intense activity, requiring control of the number of releases to avoid media saturation. In each town there was advance publicity with the SpriteBall minibus, school demonstrations by the display team and competitions, climaxing with a weekend

SpriteBall Bash, which provided a day's sport and musical entertainment as well as sampling of Sprite.

The promotion generated over six million impressions with the targeted audience, with no unfavourable comments. Unpaid broadcast time amounted to 24 minutes for radio and 3 minutes for TV, achieved with a PR budget of around $9,000. Following this success, the programme has been extended to eight other African countries.

Deciding to build a personal winning reputation is one of the most significant and enjoyable moves you can make. You will become the talk of the town, or at least of your community, and fame usually brings fortune – financial as well as personal satisfaction. You can take control of your reputation if you choose to. You can build your reputational muscles as surely as you can body-build your physical presence.

Before we move on to the step-by-step guides in Chapters 3, 4 and 5 on exactly how to strengthen your reputational bulk, here are a few words of wisdom from some people who have made it already. Celebrities, sportspeople, campaigners, whatever their territory, they have already captured the high ground.

These individuals are at the peak of their profession and have reputations that are strong and hard won. They were asked for one piece of advice that they would give to anyone looking to emulate them and build a winning reputation for themselves. Their words of wisdom are simple but very telling.

Any individual who aspires to having the level of reputational capital enjoyed by those already in the public eye should read the following comments, which were kindly submitted for this book by individuals that are already legends:

Be honest to yourself.
> STEPHEN HENDRY – EX-WORLD CHAMPION SNOOKER PLAYER

Manners cost you nothing so use them. Always be polite.
> MIKE CATT – ENGLAND RUGBY PLAYER

Never confuse fame with success.
    BRENDA BLETHYN – ACTRESS

Always think of the ramifications of what you do/say before you do/say them.
    KYRAN BRACKEN – ENGLAND RUGBY PLAYER

I believe that it is impossible to control one's reputation in the media, and especially in the press. As anyone will tell you who spends a lot of time abroad, the British press is by and large unrelentingly negative. And at least in recent years, the pressure to be rather nasty has come from the very top. Of course, it would stop immediately if the editors and proprietors were subjected to the same treatment, but they're not.

*   So I would say that it is best to avoid publicity whenever you can, and above all to refuse to give profile interviews, unless you know the journalist personally, and can believe their assurances that they are not under pressure to write negatively.*
    JOHN CLEESE – ACTOR AND WRITER

Read nothing that is written about you.
    JOANNA LUMLEY – ACTRESS

Make friends with journalists and only do live television.
    LUKE JOHNSON – CEO OF THE BELGO RESTAURANT GROUP

Never do or say anything you would not wish to see on the front page of your local weekly newspaper.

*   If you have anything to hide – don't try! Get the full story out immediately, with an apology if appropriate – or you will die the death by 1,000 cuts!*
    MARTIN BELL – UK POLITICIAN

Behave yourself.
    PHIL COLLINS – MUSICIAN

Know the answer to any question before it is asked and deliver with commitment.
    PETER MOORE – LONDON TOWN CRIER

Listen, consider and tell the truth.
    PETER JANIS – DIRECTOR GENERAL OF THE ROYAL SOCIETY FOR THE PREVENTION OF CRUELTY TO ANIMALS

Be kind to people and true to yourself.
 ELIZABETH DAWN – ACTRESS

Always show respect to the people or the club you are talking about.
 BRYAN ROBSON – MANAGER OF MIDDLESBROUGH FOOTBALL CLUB, EX-ENGLAND
 FOOTBALL CAPTAIN

*Have the courage to do what is right – always be straightforward in your
actions and make sure that everything you do will stand up to public scrutiny.*
 ROGER CATO – CEO OF HEATHROW AIRPORT

*Be honest and fair with people and help others in life, especially the sick and
old people. Always have a smile on your face.*
 DICKIE BIRD – SPORTS COMMENTATOR

*Count to 10 before answering a question from the press and treat everyone
like a human being unless they prove otherwise!*
 LYNDA BELLINGHAM – ACTRESS

Keep your own counsel, be true to yourself, keep what's precious private!
 JULIE HESMONDHALGH – ACTRESS

*Don't worry about it. Half the people like you and the other half don't: both
for fairly illogical reasons. So don't worry and be yourself.*
 MIKE ATHERTON – ENGLAND CRICKETER

Honesty is always the best policy and truth the best protection.
 SIR PADDY ASHDOWN – UK POLITICIAN, EX-LEADER OF THE LIBERAL DEMOCRATIC
 PARTY

*Don't trust journalists especially ones who seem nice. Don't respond to their
lies either. Read books not newspapers!*
 ALAN DAVIES – ACTOR AND COMEDIAN

*Find the right peg. The principle of any successful marketing/communications
strategy is finding the right voice/time and peg to hang your politics from. The
trick is to differentiate yourself from others. Putting yourself about indiscrim-
inately isn't enough.*
 OONA KING – UK POLITICIAN

Always smile – it may be hard, but try.
DAVID BELLAMY – ENVIRONMENTALIST AND SCIENTIST

Be true to yourself without promoting yourself. Spin is the enemy of promise.
JONATHAN DIMBLEBY – INTERVIEWER AND JOURNALIST

Be yourself – people in general are not stupid and recognize someone who is trying to be something other than themselves.
GARY LINEKER – SPORTS COMMENTATOR, EX-ENGLAND FOOTBALLER

If you are a lovely person who lives a blameless life there is no need for PR people or spin doctors, I've found!
HONOR BLACKMAN – ACTRESS

Be honest with everyone, especially yourself.
DAVID WEIR – FOOTBALLER

Be true to yourself and family and honest with all who you meet.
ANDY KANE – FOOTBALLER

Always be polite, even if you have to disagree/complain. Generally you're dealing with other professionals who are only trying to do their job as well. Never believe your own hype, stay grounded through old friends and family, don't be afraid to say no – there is such a thing as too much publicity!
MEERA SYAL – WRITER, ACTRESS, PLAYWRIGHT

Give your public life a focus, stick to it, and keep your private life private!
HELEN SHARMAN – FIRST BRITISH PERSON IN SPACE

Be honest, don't take yourself too seriously, and remember that no one really cares what is written about you, so if you don't either, no one cares at all (except possibly your mum and dad).
HELEN MIRREN – ACTRESS

Never be economical with the truth. You cannot fool all the people all the time.
KENNETH WOLSTENHOLME – SPORTS COMMENTATOR, COINED THE PHRASE 'THEY THINK IT'S ALL OVER … IT IS NOW' (1966 WORLD CUP)

Honour your own truth, with respect for oneself and ultimately respect for all people.

LULU – ACTRESS AND SINGER

Always present yourself well and always be courteous to people and treat people the way you like to be treated in general.

PAUL GERRARD – FOOTBALLER

Be yourself.

KOFI ANAN – SECRETARY-GENERAL, UNITED NATIONS

CHAPTER 3

Reputation as the new religion: the powers behind the movement

In this chapter we will examine the forces and trends that shape reputation. You will see that great reputations do not just happen – they are built and nurtured and we will look at how you, too, can achieve this transformation.

Quite simply, reputation management is like any other kind of management, and if you apply the traditional strategic planning cycle to reputation creation, the effects will be as dramatic as when you apply this method of thinking to any other task.

Beginning the journey to a winning reputation

Building a winning reputation will require you to think your way around a familiar planning cycle. This will take you through five key stages of thought when looking at any reputational challenges:

1. What do you want to achieve?

2. Where are you now?

3. How are you going to get there?

4. How will you evaluate progress?

5. What can you do to improve your performance continuously?

Once you accept that building a reputation is as real a task as building a house or a factory, you will see that it is not just all about image, spin and stunts. But you should also realize that this is not a task that you should handle on your own. Many people understand that reputation can be built, but most still think that this is something for the PR team alone to worry about. This thinking is at best old fashioned and unrealistic. At worst it is ostrich-like behaviour in the extreme, which can lead a company to believe that the ice it is standing on is good and thick, when in fact it is paper thin.

The truth is that business value can very easily be destroyed by disconnecting PR from reality. A house of cards, the emperor's new clothes – call it what you will – but when image and spin exceed or are totally different from reality, something bad is sure to happen sooner rather than later.

Having a good reputation is about so much more than image. Having a good reputation is all about being outstanding, not just looking outstanding. To be seen as a thought leader, you must have thought leading thoughts. To appear interesting you need actually to be interesting. You do not have the automatic right to be well thought of. You cannot buy good regard, you are not able to hire it or graft it on. Favourable opinions must be earned and won on the basis of real life achievements and qualities.

So where to start on this root and branch transformation process? First of all it is critical to understand the new environment of heightened reputation sensitivity in which all businesses and organizations find themselves. The business world has changed a great deal in the last ten years – in many ways. One of the most significant changes is the importance of reputation to commercial success. There is no doubt that reputation is one of the major new factors on the commercial horizon, which leaders from every walk of life are having to understand and manage as a matter of urgency.

There are several major drivers which have led to reputational excellence being not just an important choice, but an unstoppable prerequisite for those wishing to do business. A good reputation is increasingly becoming 'a licence to operate'. Living up to reputational expectations is no longer an option – there is a burgeoning, insatiable, world-wide demand for organizations to behave themselves and promote their activities in a transparent, engaging way. Today, business needs the permission of governments, the people and watchdogs simply to trade. Any moves into new areas – geographic or product related – need a further stamp of public approval on the corporate passport.

In the past, companies and products only had to meet standards for safety and manufacturing compliance before they reached the market. Today there is another requirement, which is to pass the reputation tests applied by stakeholders, who need – demand even – to know about and 'approve' of company actions and new developments. Even beyond simple awareness, the outside world expects companies to open their souls and minds to provide opinions and comments, support and contributions back into society. It is no longer enough for a company to simply be in society, it must be part of society and seen to be playing an active role.

Whose reputation is it anyway?

So what is going on to make this area of reputation management so important to so many companies and organizations? In my research into global reputation management trends, I have identified eight factors that companies need to consider when developing a reputation management plan:

1. Stakeholder convergence and the need for cohesion

2. Power of the people

3. Total media spotlight

4. Globalization

5. Crisis explosion

6. Good corporate citizenship

7. Growing importance of reputation to business

8. The Internet.

Let us take a look at each driver and think about what it means for those of us who want to create and run a winning reputation programme to boost business and personal career success.

Stakeholder convergence and the need for cohesion

Today there are no longer two sides to every coin. This is because we are seeing the rapid convergence of stakeholders' interests and the growth of a more holistic view of businesses and brands in society. In the past, PR was simpler. There were still lots of audiences but they all kept themselves to themselves, which meant that you could segment your communications very easily. You told your consumers what they wanted to hear, you told the financial community what they wanted to know and you told your staff as little as possible. Each communication channel was discrete, relationships were intimate and there was no real migration of information between stakeholders.

This was very neat and tidy. Such clear segmentation meant that you could quite safely brag to shareholders about your huge profits, while at the same time talking to consumers about how low your prices were. Companies could pay lower rates in one country than in another because nobody would ever make such international comparisons. Controversial ingredients or labour policies could be applied in parts of the world where the searchlight of publicity and media scrutiny never ventured forth.

And even if people did notice the occasional anomaly or conflict, the media and other observers retained a deference to those in positions of power, so that most cases were either not dealt with as high profile or were simply accepted without remark.

Also, this absence of stakeholder overlap meant that it did not really matter if you chose not to communicate with certain groups at all. Keeping out of the way of opponents or difficult or apparently powerless audiences was often the best policy for a quiet reputational life.

That was then. The world is now a much smaller place and that means you need a bigger view. Today everything is on show all the time to all the people. This is what I refer to as stakeholder convergence. The truth is that there are no longer separate stakeholder groups. Everybody is interested in everything. There is one population made up of special interest groups with, as you might expect, special areas of interest. However, all the groups overlap and are linked, so that communications must be distinct and integrated at the same time.

The overall watchword for this type of loose/tight reputation management across micro and macro audiences, at the same time and everywhere, is *cohesion*. To build a winning reputation, you need to adopt a cohesive approach to ensure that you do not drop any of the juggling balls and that your message plays well regardless of who or where it is being delivered. These changes in stakeholder composition and interaction are shown in Figure 3.1.

The true picture is that we all wear many hats and refuse to be put into tidy audience groups any longer. Somewhere along the line, the different audience groups have started to talk to each other and have stopped seeing the world in neat little packages relating only to one's peers. Woe betide any communications professional who misses this change and continues to try and divide and rule. Today the need is to bring a holistic approach to the process of communication – united your reputation will stand, divided it will fall.

The obsolescence of putting audiences in boxes becomes apparent when you stop to think about what real life is like for us all in today's connected, hyper-mediated environment. For example, consumers do not just buy your products, they also:

- Buy your competitor's products

- Vote

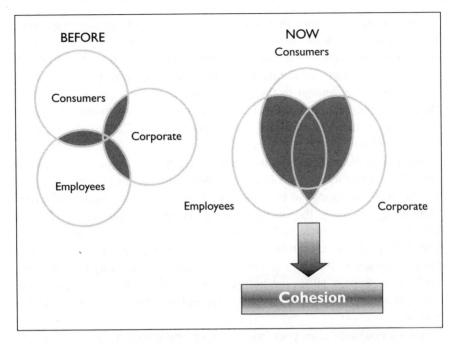

Figure 3.1 Converging stakeholder interests

- Invest
- Work
- Live in a community
- Travel
- Influence decisions
- Make decisions
- Lead people
- Follow people.

As you can see, a typical consumer participates in a wide range of activities, many of which can impact on your business. And it is not only this group: politicians, fund managers, business leaders, employees, charities, suppliers and all the other stakeholder groups also do some or all of the above list, in addition to their main area of activity.

The world viewpoint on reputation is increasingly an aggregate one, taking many elements into account, and your communications must reflect the new set of glasses that everyone is wearing today. To be seen in the round, you must communicate in the round and deliver a cohesive set of messages that appeal to the specific needs of each group, but which support each other rather than conflict. An impressive example of this co-ordination of messages to all stakeholder groups is Case Study 10.10 of Unilever's launch of Persil detergent tablets.

Once you observe this convergence, it becomes apparent why it is reputational suicide to miss out any stakeholder group. For example, let us say that you choose to convince the public about the merits of a new technology by using the third-party endorsement of the media. This is clearly a good plan. Detailed and well-targeted media briefings can certainly grab the attention of journalists. A clever press pack and a good interview will have them with their pens poised ready to write up a high profile report. However, before they do, they will do what any good journalist would do and contact independent experts in the field for a view.

So, immediately after your briefing, they could well be on the phone to industry observers such as financial analysts, scientists, research institutes, or political contacts to get their view on 'this new development'. If you have failed to brief these informed experts in advance – even if the sin is one of omission rather than deliberate exclusion – you are likely to get a beating.

At best, the fact that the other audiences have not come across your new development will mean that they will have nothing to say to amplify your own promotional activity. This is a real lost opportunity. A pre-briefed independent expert can provide highly valuable third-party commentary and even endorsement, as seen in Case Study 10.24. Most expert observers will be flattered that you have pre-briefed them on your new story, and therefore they are likely to be favourable. Leave them out and there is a risk that the call from the journalist will embarrass and annoy them.

At worst they will lash out and make an unhelpful remark, probably without any basis in fact. Often they simply do not have a view, but, furious at being 'caught out' and conscious that their fame is partly due to the ability to come up with pithy commentary, their reaction will often resort to glib, eye-catching criticism. PR abhors a vacuum and, when genuine information is lacking, the canny industry observer will speculate in an idle but still cutting manner to fill the media void, and notch up another memorable quotation for the cuttings book.

The PR professional who misses an audience is missing a trick. What is more, they are running the strong risk that all their good work will be undermined. Possibly one of the most high profile examples of where omitting an audience group has led to commercial catastrophe is the case of genetically modified organisms (GMOs) in Europe. Companies involved in developing technologies in this field – most notably Monsanto – were so convinced of the merits of GMOs that they went straight to the European public to tell them how great GMOs were going to be for society. Breathtakingly (looking back), Monsanto embarked on a lavish corporate advertising campaign, telling us how GM food would cure world hunger, provide us with cheaper, tastier food, reduce the use of pesticides and deliver all manner of other wonders for our society.

The trouble with this approach was that the relevant informed communities – scientists, food experts, politicians, aid agencies, food and nutrition journalists – had not been approached first. There was no bedrock of understanding among the opinion forming audience and, as a result, the high profile campaign was built only on the hired sands of advertising.

So when the bemused public turned to the experts for advice and commentary, the media and other observers were not ready. Monsanto had not primed them sufficiently. As a result, the journalists and many others were as nonplussed by Monsanto's ideas as everyone else. The difference was that this community held the passwords to power in terms of the reputation battle. Without their support and credible endorsement, the seeds of the GMO debate were never going to germinate, no matter how much work the scientists had put in.

The questions were many – for years we have all read that world hunger is less to do with the ability to grow food and more to do with distribution difficulties. According to the United Nations Food and Agricultural Organisation, if all the food produced in the world were divided equally, every man, woman and child would consume 2,760 calories per day. How were GM crops going to tackle this (unless they had been genetically modified to have legs so they could distribute themselves)?

Another obvious point missed was that Europe had been through one food scare after another: BSE, or mad cow disease, *E. coli*, listeria. Controversial ingredients and unhealthy eating trends had all contributed to a loss of faith among European consumers in intensive agricultural practices that produced cheap, but low quality, or even dangerous, foods which were often perceived as 'unnatural'. The last thing people were interested in was more science in food production.

Instead, people were looking for more naturally produced food. The cost savings achieved by European postwar food production advances were now seen as a price not worth paying if those low prices brought with them the risks associated with intensive agri/industrial production.

Promoting GMOs in Europe was always going to be difficult, but it need not have been the PR and commercial disaster that it turned out to be. If Monsanto had simply applied the classic planning cycle to the communication of this new innovation, recognized the interconnection and closeness of stakeholder groups and the need to manage them cohesively, it is possible that GMOs would still have a healthy future, rather than being very much on the reputation back foot.

As it stands, GMOs have the PR black spot of death on them and perhaps the world will ultimately lose out on many of the undoubted benefits that these developments could have brought us, if they had been presented in a constructive manner.

While a cohesive approach is essential in order to achieve a winning reputation, there are some exceptions to the rule of audience inclusion. For example, sometimes there can be a product or an issue, where the views of the public differ from the views of the expert observers in the field. If this is the case, observers such as specialist journalists or industry experts can actually be very damaging to a reputation if they are included fully, especially if they are the first group to be communicated with, as is normally the case with most reputation management campaigns.

For example, this often happens in areas such as wine or automobiles or in relation to specific films, foods, books or holiday destinations. If your business is involved in the promotion of mass-market items, these are often given short shrift by the informed intelligentsia who write about or comment on your particular area of business. So if your trade is making popular, but essentially commonplace, family run-around automobiles, you are likely to be portrayed as dull in the 'go faster' motoring journals, although you may be beloved by the housewife and the senior citizen.

Toyota's Corolla is the bestselling car in the world, yet I have never read a review of the Corolla in any auto magazine that is overtly complimentary. Yes, they acknowledge that it is well built and reliable, but appealing? Never! Sexy? No way!

Books and films can suffer a similar fate. It is unlikely that the latest potboiler novel is about to win plaudits from the literary reviewers, even though it may sell millions of copies in airports all over the world. A new blockbuster film may be panned by the critics but can still fill our cinemas if the stars and the special effects do their stuff.

In these cases, when you are faced with a hostile or irrelevant media or group of expert observers traditionally dealing with your product area, there are a number of options:

- Exclude them from your communications

- Build relationships with a new set of journalists who do appreciate your products, for example forget the motoring journalists and target the lifestyle writers

- Bypass the media totally and use direct communications, for example the Internet, customer events, direct mail and word of mouth endorsement campaigns.

While these approaches are relevant in many areas, for the majority of cases a holistic approach to communicating with stakeholder groups is the safest, surest way of building a winning reputation. Cohesion in communications is almost always the key to success and is more important as stakeholder convergence becomes an increasingly powerful driver in the need to improve reputation management.

This is why it is vital not to leave out an audience on the reputation building party invite list. But who should be on the list? Who are the movers and shakers and who are merely the gentle stirrers? Table 3.1 shows the principal audiences that should be considered in any reputation management campaign. This provides a useful checklist to help you to think about your own business against each audience. How well do you know the people that matter to your business in each category? Do you have their names and addresses on a central file? How often do you communicate with them? Do you know what each group is saying about you and your company? These are all questions to which you should know the answers for every audience group.

You will have been gainfully employed if you spend some time identifying the individuals and organizations in those categories that you need to get close to or at least to be aware of. Once you have compiled that magical list, you will need to develop a plan of action for each audience, and even for specific individuals within each group.

Table 3.1 Who matters to your business?

Market	Owners	Community	Organizations
Consumers	Stockholders	Legislators	Industry leaders
Competitors	Financial community	Opinion leaders	Employees
Distributors		Society	Unions
Suppliers			

You also need to think about why they matter to your business. How do you best communicate with them? What do they want to know about? What are their interests? What publications do they read? How can you reach them and what do you want to say to them?

It is important not to let anyone or anything slip through the PR net and over the next few chapters we will look at how you can go about making your reputation vessel totally seaworthy for the voyage of self-promotion.

As well as missing an audience, it is also unwise to be selective in the issues you address and how they are managed in relation to each audience. For example, consumers no longer simply want the cheapest and the best quality product. Assuming that that is all they are interested in is dangerous and blinkered.

In fact, today's consumer is looking for the company that produces what they buy to provide more than a simple product. Increasingly they are looking behind the brand and the products to scrutinize the behaviour and reputation of the company that produces or sells them the item. In fact, in many cases the brand is becoming secondary to the company that makes it. Think of McDonald's and you think as much about the company as you do the brand. Similarly with Nike, Gap, Shell, the corporate reputation is a significant component of the brand value, to such an extent that they are one and the same thing.

Some new research carried out by Weber Shandwick has explored this change in world-wide consumer attitudes a little further. In January 2001 research was carried out with 8,000 consumers in Australia, Belgium, France, Great Britain, Italy, Singapore, Spain and the United States. Two groups of consumers were questioned. First a representative sample of the 'everyday consumer', then what we call 'leading-edge consumers'. These are typically those consumers who are more highly educated, socially upmarket and with a heightened awareness of issues in society. Often they are politically active or play a role in their local communities in some active way. Typically leading-edge consumers represent around 10% of a national population.

The objective of the research was to test how much issues traditionally thought of as 'corporate', and of no real interest to consumers, were coming into the field of vision of the consumer when selecting a brand. In particular, we wanted to see what issues mattered the most and how these were affecting people's brand consumption behaviour. In other words, do corporate issues make a difference when it comes to choosing goods in the supermarket?

Up until now, the view was that there was very little crossover. It was acknowledged that people may be more aware of issues such as animal testing, child labour or environmental concerns, but at the end of the day, they still buy whatever is cheapest, the best quality or simply the brand they trust.

The fact is that convergence of stakeholders' interests has applied to consumers as much as anywhere else, and this new research shows that consumers are thinking more corporately. They still rate price and quality as the number one priority when it comes to selecting a product to buy, but they are also interested in other factors such as how the company that makes the product is behaving, how it treats its workforce, does it use child labour, are there perpetual cases of industrial dispute, does it do its bit in the community, is it environmentally responsible and so on.

We also asked consumers if it was important for the company behind the brand to be a local company from that country. So much vitriol is addressed at 'faceless multinationals' that we wanted to explore the drivers behind this way of thinking. Do consumers, we wondered, prefer home-grown goods to the progeny of globalization?

The results were fascinating for anyone looking to present a balanced, cohesive communications campaign in order to sell products to the consumer. It showed that all these social/corporate considerations carried some weight, making it clear that those brands which recognized this as a route to differentiation could reap substantial rewards.

Second, the results showed that, not surprisingly, the 'leading-edge consumers' rated wider social issues more highly than the average consumer. While this result is not startling, it is nonetheless useful, as it indicates which issues matter to this group. They can be helpful for those developing communications plans that need to target this discrete segment of consumers.

The one result that did surprise my team and I was the lack of impor-tance placed on the nationality of the company. With the exception of Australia and Spain, consumers did not feel that it was especially impor-tant to their buying habits if the company behind the product was local to their country.

After reading these surprising results, I reflected on the countless PR campaigns designed to demonstrate that a multinational company is 'part of the local community' and wondered just how valuable this route had been. It seems that today's consumer has accepted globalization and will take the best that the world has to offer, as opposed to clinging to patriotic buying habits, simply to fly the flag.

The results from two European and one Asian country, Australia and the US are shown in more detail in Figures 3.2–3.6, first for all consumers, then for 'leading-edge consumers'.

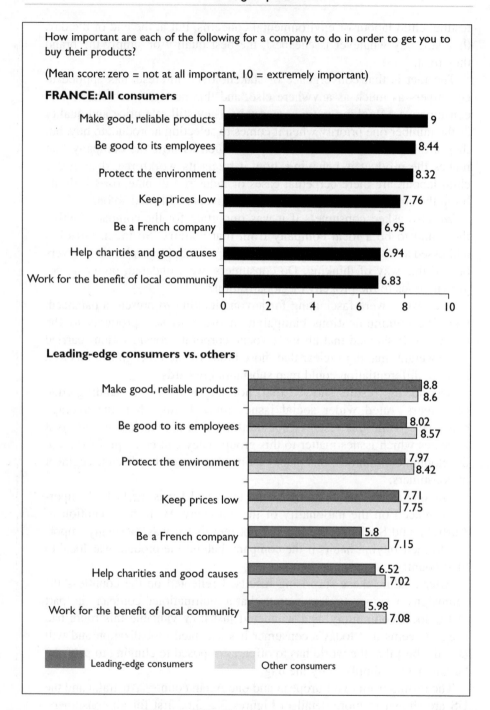

Figure 3.2 Consumers becoming corporate – results of research in France

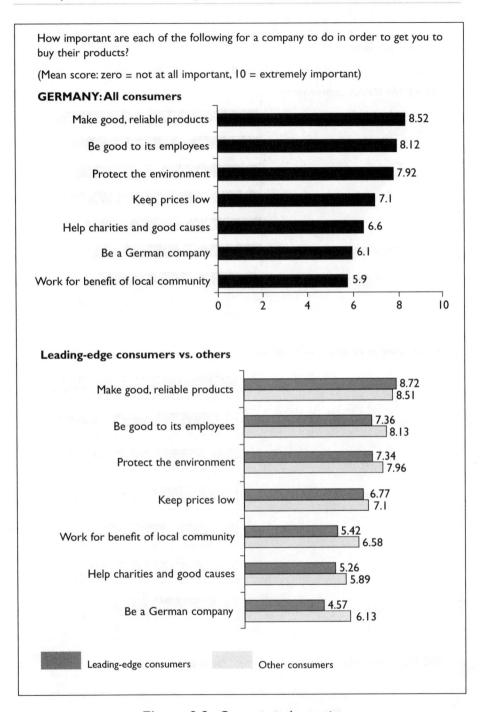

Figure 3.3 Consumers becoming
corporate – results of research in Germany

Winning Reputations

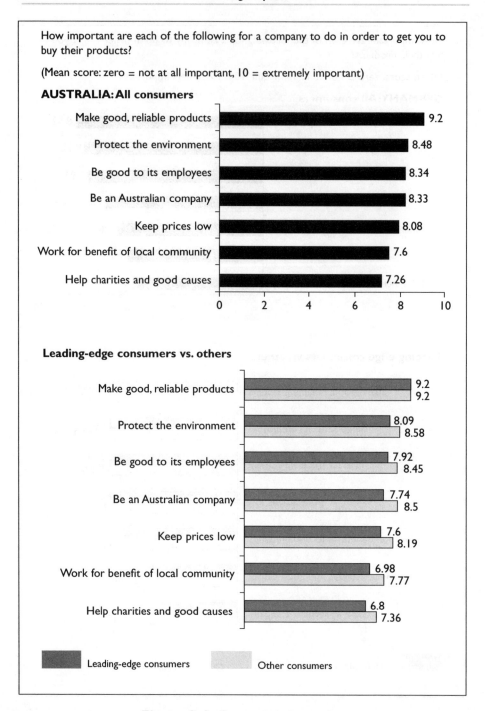

Figure 3.4 Consumers becoming
corporate – results of research in Australia

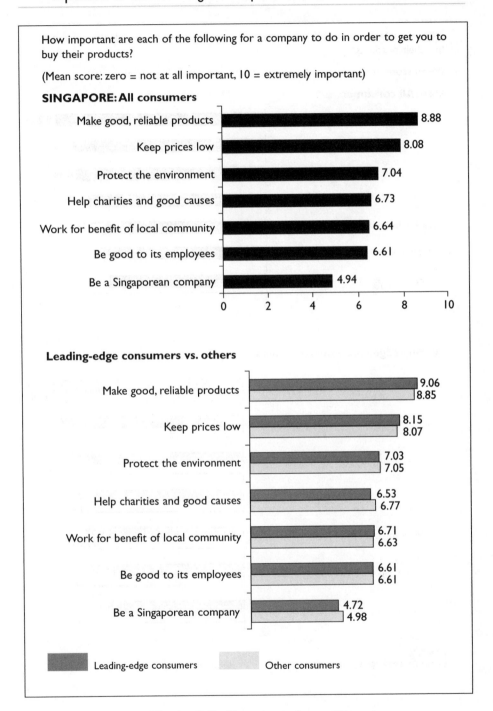

Figure 3.5 Consumers becoming
corporate – results of research in Singapore

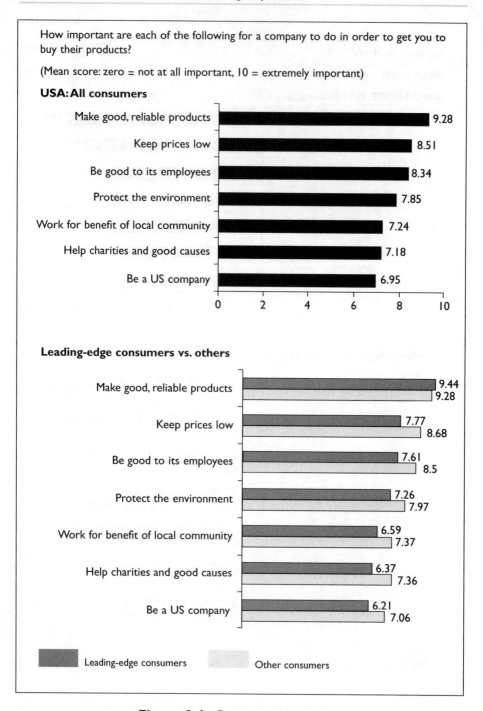

How important are each of the following for a company to do in order to get you to buy their products?

(Mean score: zero = not at all important, 10 = extremely important)

USA: All consumers

Make good, reliable products	9.28
Keep prices low	8.51
Be good to its employees	8.34
Protect the environment	7.85
Work for benefit of local community	7.24
Help charities and good causes	7.18
Be a US company	6.95

Leading-edge consumers vs. others

	Leading-edge consumers	Other consumers
Make good, reliable products	9.44	9.28
Keep prices low	7.77	8.68
Be good to its employees	7.61	8.5
Protect the environment	7.26	7.97
Work for benefit of local community	6.59	7.37
Help charities and good causes	6.37	7.36
Be a US company	6.21	7.06

Figure 3.6 Consumers becoming corporate – results of research in the USA

Table 3.2 How stakeholders are converging

Admired attributes of a company/brand	Ranking Business/opinion formers	Consumers
Consumer focus	1	1
Quality products/services	2	2
Believability	3	3
Attracts/keeps best talent	4	4
Responds to change	5	5
Good financial performer	6	9

A similar survey by Burson-Marsteller in 1998 echoes the point made in our research about the convergence of stakeholder groups. In its survey the priorities of consumers are compared to those of business leaders and opinion formers. As can be seen in Table 3.2, the interests are the same for both groups, despite their apparently disparate natures. Interestingly though, the one area of disagreement is 'Good financial performance' as an admired attribute. Perhaps not surprisingly, consumers still rate this very lowly when considering the reputation of a company, while business leaders give it a higher rating. However, as the ownership of stocks and shares widens to include more consumers, this view seems likely to change.

Power of the people

Being consumer led is now the norm for companies, organizations and governments in most countries of the world. Even former soviet countries have turned from command economies and societies to consumer-led models. Governments base policies on focus groups. Newspapers and TV networks produce material designed to grab readership figures and ratings. Companies are obsessed more than ever not only with consumer research, but with consumer feedback and dialogue. Helplines, Internet contact sites and telephone service centres are some of the fastest growth areas in terms of customer service and marketing spend. If consumers want something, institutions and businesses increasingly understand that it makes good business and political sense to offer it.

As well as giving people want they want, companies now will not give them what they don't want. For example, companies choose to stop selling products which they know are perfectly safe or superior in performance, if the public loses faith in them or stubbornly refuses to accept what is on offer. At the end of the day business exists to give the consumer what she or he wants, whatever the rights and wrongs might be. Similarly, governments need to win and keep voters if they are to exist at all; it is a foolish politician that loses touch with the people who vote him or her into office.

For those companies that do not deliver the highest levels of customer responsiveness, there are a plethora of consumer rights groups, media watchdogs and aggressive consumer affairs minded politicians who will help to whip up consumer fury and focus the glare of publicity to ensure that the customer gets whatever support it takes to put the offending company or organization back into its place.

There is no doubt that this consumer power has had a dramatic effect on companies and institutions, mainly for the good. For example, companies can no longer get away with shoddy customer service, and fierce competition in most sectors typically means that companies must keep on their toes. This has had major implications for those involved in the management of reputation. At the very least it has meant that every company must devote some resources to the relentless stream of journalist enquiries, consumer requests for information, complaint handling and satisfaction delivery.

Expectations are high and if these aspects of external communications are handled poorly any company will quickly feel the wrath of the people and their popular media champions, often backed up by political supporters of the consumer super race.

Total media spotlight

Closely linked to the driver of people power is the existence of a new type of media that is totally global, instant and relentless in its drive to dig deeper and deeper to find sensationalism. There is very little reverence, respect or even trust in the media for business. Stories whizz around the world like viruses. International comparisons mean that any inconsistency in a company's policies or activities are easily revealed.

A story in one country is now frequently used to fuel the media in another part of the world. This means that companies need to be well organized to deal with media activity internationally. It is essential that early warning systems exist so that all countries are aware of potentially damaging news stories breaking in one part of the world. It is critical therefore to have proper statements prepared and capable of being distributed at speed so that the organization is not caught napping.

A simple guideline would be to assume that whatever is currently only in your corporate mind will eventually become common knowledge. The media will find out – eventually. And if the truth will out, it is therefore crucial to be on the front foot and ready to respond and pre-empt wherever possible.

Globalization

Globalization has accelerated the move towards more emphasis on reputation management as a serious priority for business. Some of this sentiment has been as a result of companies adopting a more global approach to all their business functions and including PR in this housekeeping exercise. Many have simply looked at ways to develop and apply consistent PR policies across the world. But for most companies this is just the start of how they need to reframe their reputation management processes as a result of 'going global'.

For example, globalization presents all sorts of new issues to be managed. Globalization is not always a popular fact of life and many multinational corporations place a great deal of communications emphasis in talking about their contribution to local communities and giving the impression of being part of the country in which they operate, in order to offset the negative associations with homogeneous business cultures across the globe.

In many cases, this facsimile of a local positioning has been achieved very effectively. In several countries, brands such as Heinz, Kellogg and Ford are seen as part of the national fabric of life. However, for some brands this never seems to happen. I am sure that no matter how local they try to be, brands such as McDonald's, Coca-Cola and Boeing will always be part of the American dream and Sony, Toyota and Nikon will forever be linked with Japanese technical excellence, regardless of where the goods are manufactured.

But, as we have seen from the earlier research into consumer purchasing behaviour, the 'localness' of a company is perhaps a reputation trigger that has been overplayed by overly sensitive multinationals who would prefer to be multilocal citizens of the world, rather than play on their national heritage, which can have a far more old-fashioned and racially loaded feel as a positioning.

While this is only one study, perhaps it indicates that, for most consumers, being local is relatively unimportant. In fact, consumers want their cameras and electronic goods to be from Japan because that is where the most prestigious brands tend to come from. Coca-Cola should be an American icon because, perhaps, that is a major part of its appeal.

Crisis explosion

Linked to people power, the rise in pressure groups and an accompanying aggressive media is the rapid rise in crises affecting the reputations of companies. A crisis and the less explosive but still highly toxic issues that often hover around businesses are great drivers of reputation improvement and vigilance as well as a huge drain on resources.

A company crisis can bring your company to a standstill, but handled well it can build your reputation back up to a higher level than before the incident. This is vividly illustrated in the case studies of P&O's handling of its *Aurora* crisis (Case Study 10.25) and The Body Shop's management of its hemp campaign (Case Study 2.2). What is clear is that every company should be ready for the worst. Employee disputes, lawsuits, consumer complaints that turn sour, factories emitting pollution, and products that have to be recalled are just some of the everyday disasters that need to be managed by the reputation protection team.

These events are as frequent as ever but, notably, the media coverage of them is rising and is invariably international. The stakes are higher and the result is more work for those looking to build, but also protect, winning reputations.

Good corporate citizenship

The tendency for companies to work with good causes, and the expectation from the public and governments for them to do so, is another factor to be considered when planning a reputation management programme. Research consistently shows that around 80% of consumers are willing to purchase a specific product if it is linked with supporting a good cause, as long as there is parity of quality and price with similar products. This has led to a huge rise in areas such as cause-related marketing (as shown in Case Study 10.23 of Persil's linkage with the UK charity Comic Relief), where companies donate a percentage of sales to a charity, and to other examples of companies generally supporting good causes with donations, but also in local communities through schemes such as employee volunteering projects.

More and more multinationals are turning to good causes as a way of differentiating themselves and building affection for the company and its brands. Recently, for example, both Coca-Cola and Microsoft have committed huge funds to Aids research in Africa. This type of self-enlightened corporate philanthropy is escalating in popularity and is another reason behind the boom that we are seeing in reputation management.

Growing importance of reputation to business

Not only does the outside world think that reputation counts for something, but the need to manage perception has also caught the imagination of senior management world-wide. A recent survey showed that 64% of global CEOs now see PR as more important than advertising in building reputation capital. And 67% say that reputation is one of their company's most important assets, equal to, or even above, strong earnings.

This surge of top level endorsement has fuelled the reputation management revolution that we have seen in recent years. Not only has it seen the release of adequate funding, but such high level commitment has ensured that PR and reputation become far more integrated into the overall business goals of an organization and move higher up the corporate agenda, often usurping advertising, marketing and investor relations as the drivers of external relations strategies.

The Internet

The full implications of the Internet to those managing reputation is dealt with in Chapter 8, but suffice it to say here that the primary impact that the Internet has had on reputation management is that it has created more work for PR practitioners.

The Internet is yet another conduit that needs maintaining and policing. On a more positive note, it makes communications – especially directly to stakeholders – far easier. In a recent survey, just under 50% of major corporations felt that the net made reputation management easier. The only area of the net that seems to cause great concern is chat rooms, with 39% saying that this was the area they as PR people feared the most.

Whatever you make of the net, you cannot ignore it and there is no doubt that it creates a whole new impetus and requirement for companies to be more professional and active about their PR performance, a topic that will be explored in more detail in Chapter 8.

Understanding these major changes in the world and the implications that they have for how you manage your commercial and personal reputation is the vital first step in taking control of how you are seen by those that matter to you.

By understanding the transparent and instant environment in which we all have to operate, you will be well placed to move on to the next stage, which is how you turn that knowledge of the system into a plan that creates strong PR armour for a thin-skinned world.

CHAPTER 4

Your reputation architecture: a blueprint for a winning reputation

In the last chapter we looked at why there is a greater need in today's business environment to be more communicative to both the outside and inside worlds. This chapter will look at how to go about it.

As we have seen, good reputations are not just skin deep. To make reputation really work for you it needs to become part of your DNA, but how does the committed reputation engineer go about altering his reputational genes?

PR and reputation management are often seen as black arts, but in reality there is no reason why PR and reputation cannot be managed in the same way as any other aspect of business.

In recent years a number of initiatives have taken place to attempt to formulize the PR and reputation management process. Leading PR consultants around the world, along with academics and one or two management consultancies, have looked at what constitutes best practice in reputation management and attempted to interpret the latest thinking into management tools.

Especially over the last four to five years, it has become increasingly clear that business people are looking for a more systematic way to manage their reputation. This reflects the growing recognition of the importance of reputation management and a realization that the consequences of not managing this aspect of the business professionally are too serious to be ignored or handled in an amateurish manner.

It was for these reasons that I began to set down a blueprint for managing reputation which I then used with a number of multinational clients. Working for a major consultancy with offices around the world, I have been able to draw on research and case studies from a wide range of industries and national and international scenarios.

I have also benefited from time spent with academics working in this field, experienced PR colleagues around the world and several client organizations, who have all been very helpful in my quest to set out a road map for those wishing to travel on the reputation journey from obscurity to celebrity.

The approach I have developed and have been applying with my clients over recent years in order to create winning reputations, I refer to as 'reputation architecture'. Like brand architecture, much of the thinking behind reputation architecture is based on best practice and research already carried out in the industry.

The difference between existing reputation management models and the reputation architecture approach is that the process I have developed is action orientated – rather than simply diagnostic – and is equally applicable to an individual as to a multinational business.

Reputation architecture building takes existing reputation management models to a deeper level by encouraging an organization or an individual to change the way they are in order to improve their reputation, rather than simply working at a cosmetic level that focuses on communications rather than content. Reputation architecture is about building a better business, not simply a better reputation.

Engineering a healthy PR genome

Let us now take a step-by-step look at the phases involved in reputation architecture. The goal is the creation of an organization where a winning reputation is part of the character and values of the business. Organizations that develop a robust reputation architecture and live within it will establish a winning reputation PR genome which will characterize the organization. This winning reputation PR genome can be seen as a simple planning tool for maintaining and building a genetic difference in your business compared to your competitors.

So what might this PR genome look like under the microscope? Figure 4.1 shows its structure and how the interdependent elements of reputation management combine to create the basic building blocks of a healthy PR life.

The PR genome is a useful sketch of the pathway to attaining a good reputation. It is a journey which requires businesses and individuals to assess how they are seen, how they want to be seen and what they need to change to obtain their goals. It is a root and branch review process. The PR genome also shows that for those committed to improving their reputation the benefits are more than superficial. By determining to improve your reputation for real, you will also be improving the way you work, the way your business operates and the values by which it lives. If this truly happens, you can see that PR really can make the world a better place.

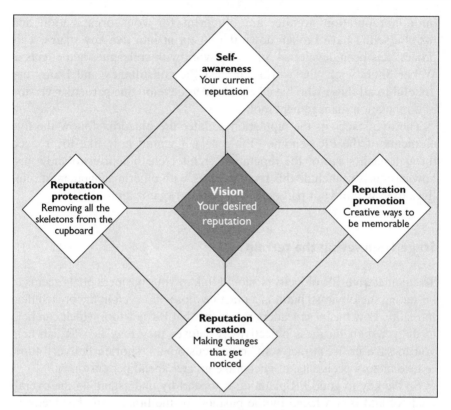

Figure 4.1 The PR genome

This is a journey that will be stimulating and challenging, but certainly one that can be made successfully by anyone with the humility to listen and the self-confidence to take on the persona of an inspirational leader, with the reputational high life that goes with it.

In the following pages we will look at the simple steps that business people need to follow in order to breathe life into each element of the PR genome; to make their reputation a living, vital force behind their business and personal success.

Five key stages of the reputation architecture blueprint

Let us now look at the elements within the PR genome and move from this micro level to a macro level and see how we can start with the genome to build a reputation architecture blueprint for your organization and for yourself. I have broken down the blueprint into five key stages. This process has been developed following work with colleagues and clients at Weber Shandwick, the world's largest PR consultancy and I am very grateful to all those who have helped me to develop this particular version of a reputation management tool.

The five stages of the reputation architecture blueprint follow the five elements of the PR genome (Table 4.1). I would now like to proceed through each stage of the reputation architecture blueprint to show just how easy it is to include this process along with other management disciplines used within your particular business or organization.

Stage 1: surveying the terrain

To say that your PR objectives should link to your business goals seems to be stating the obvious, but it is a practice more observed in the breach than in reality. Few business leaders recognize that PR is a tool which can help to deliver their business objectives, whatever they may be. PR can help you to save costs, attract staff, retain customers, shorten delivery time, reduce factory accidents, or encourage greater spend per customer.

So the key to good PR planning is to start by understanding the overall goals of and issues faced by the business or the brand. Another factor to work from is the overall mission and vision of the organization. While the goals of the business provide you with the direction, the mission and vision provide you with the personality.

Far too often, PR people have no idea what the overall goals of the business are; or if they are aware of the goals, they do not knit them totally into their PR programme. Not only does it make good business sense to link business and PR goals, but it also makes sense from a career point of view.

Table 4.1 Five stages of the reputation architechture blueprint

Element of the PR genome	Stage of the reputation architecture blueprint
Self-awareness	Surveying the terrain
Vision	Sketching the finished building
Reputation protection	Safe foundations
Reputation promotion	Structural strength
Reputation creation	Ongoing maintenance

It will be far more compelling to explain that your PR budget is supporting the same goals set by the CEO.

Once the business challenges are established, the next step is to be clear about the mission and vision of the PR team itself in relation to supporting the business.

Let us look first of all at how to develop the mission and vision that needs to be established for the PR team and programme. Below is the mission established by the PR team at one large company, who felt that their key role was to integrate the ways that different areas of the business were managing communications:

> Bringing a cohesive communications strategy across previously disconnected channels to proactively manage the external agenda, adding value to the business.

The PR team spent time reviewing the existing communications structure, plan and resources in order to develop this raison d'être. Having a focus such as this can prove helpful, not only for the work of the PR team, but also for explaining to others within the organization the role of the PR function.

Another recommendation to help to knit the PR activity into the fabric of the business overall is to involve people other than PR practitioners when developing the communications plan. One suggestion is to set up a 'reputation consultative group' of senior representatives from around the business to act as a team of advisors when agreeing on communications priorities and tone for the PR plan. Representatives from legal, technical, marketing, finance, IT, manufacturing and research are all areas that could be usefully involved in such a group.

There are many benefits to including a wide range of representatives from around the organization:

- Asking these individuals about their priorities and getting them to think about how PR can help them will often be a new experience that will open their eyes to the benefits of PR

- By involving non-PR people you will be able to embed your PR activity into the fabric of the business, so that the PR becomes part of the business, not something that happens in isolation

- Non-PR people can bring a truly fresh perspective on how the business communicates

▪ It is an opportunity to educate colleagues on the limitations and value of PR and the importance of reputation management to the total business success

▪ The process will help to improve the chances of the PR activity being supported by colleagues from across the business

▪ Colleagues from around the organization can highlight key issues and areas of strength which will be very valuable ammunition for PR exploitation later on, once the programme is up and running.

It is recommended that the reputation consultative group meet on a quarterly basis at least in order to review the PR programme and check that the group still feels that the PR activity is serving the needs of the business or organization as it should.

This simple planning stage is fairly common in many organizations, but the involvement of non-PR senior management in developing the PR plan is rarely used. This involvement of senior colleagues acting as nonexecutive directors to the PR team can pay considerable dividends as the business becomes hot wired to the PR function.

Stage 2: sketching the finished building

Once the senior PR team knows where they are going and have the blessing of the rest of the business, the next stage is to develop a detailed plan of how the finished reputation identikit will look. There are three steps to building your unique reputation identikit, and these are:

▪ Reputation assessment

▪ Audience prioritising and role definition

▪ Winning friends and winning reputations.

Reputation assessment

This phase is all about taking the current reputation temperature of the business. You need to understand what the outside world thinks of you and your business, how the media sees you, how the business sees itself and how you and your business are stacking up against the competitors, in general and specifically in terms of being a provider of PR materials. There are three main dimensions that need to be considered:

1. Corporate reputation – the reputation that you have as a business or an organization

2. Peer reputation – your standing within your particular business sector or area of operation

3. Brand reputation – attitudes towards what you sell, your product or service, or point of view (if you are a campaigning organization).

It is useful to think of your reputation on these three levels as one overall picture, as there is, as we have seen, greater convergence between stakeholder groups and the elements of an organization's reputation. People are increasingly looking at the corporations that bring them famous brands and seeing the full picture. That is why it is essential to understand and manage all aspects of an organization's reputation in an integrated, holistic way.

To establish how you stand versus your competitors in these three areas you must research among those groups of people that matter to your business. Here are some suggestions on how you might go about this vital task.

Corporate reputation

The task here is to benchmark yourself against companies or organizations in general to see how you stand. This is an area where a fair amount of existing work exists. Several studies have been completed over recent years which have asked the public and opinion formers what they take into account when they consider the reputation of a company or organization. For example, every year publications such as *Fortune* magazine, the *Financial Times* and *Management Today* in the UK all run reputation surveys which look at broadly the same criteria (Table 4.2).

All the criteria in Table 4.2 focus on the views of the opinion formers, such as politicians, senior business leaders, financial analysts, business journalists and so on. This is a well-informed group that will be able to give sensible answers to how major corporations are perceived in areas such as financial management, strategic vision and so on.

However, the general public's view of a corporation is becoming more influential and, as we have seen, their priorities are increasingly the same as those of opinion formers. For example, it is surprising to see how traditional opinion formers, such as politicians and financial analysts, are as concerned today with reputational issues such as ethical business or environmental sustainability as consumer groups.

Table 4.2 *Fortune*, the *Financial Times* and *Management Today* corporate reputation criteria			
Publication	**Criteria used to assess reputation**	**Audience researched**	**Criteria for inclusion**
Fortune magazine	■ Quality of management ■ Quality of products/services ■ Innovation ■ Long-term investment value ■ Financial soundness ■ Employee talent ■ Social responsibility ■ Use of corporate assets	Opinion formers	Major global corporations
Financial Times	■ Strong strategy ■ Quality of products and services ■ Maximizing customer satisfaction ■ Successful change management and globalization ■ Business leadership ■ Innovation ■ Robust and humane corporate culture	CEOs and opinion formers	European companies listed in European stock exchanges
Management Today	■ Quality of management ■ Ability to attract/retain talent ■ Quality of marketing ■ Financial soundness ■ Value as a long-term investment ■ Environmental responsibility ■ Quality of products and services ■ Capacity to innovate ■ Use of corporate assets	CEOs and opinion formers	UK companies listed in London Stock Exchange

For this reason, Weber Shandwick commissioned some new research four years ago which is regularly updated and combines the traditional opinion formers' views with those of the general public. The research is carried out by Professor Charles Fombrun of the New York University Stern Business School. Initially the research was completed in the US, but plans are in place to repeat it world-wide. Essentially the study seeks to define and track those factors that the public and opinion formers consider when forming a view of the reputation of a company or a brand.

The results showed that a number of factors were important, which Professor Fombrun then clustered into six principal drivers of reputation as shown in Figure 4.2. These six drivers of reputation, or a combination of the ones used by the *Financial Times*, *Fortune* or *Management Today*, can provide a very helpful set of criteria against which you can judge your corporate reputation.

Peer reputation

While it is useful to judge yourself against all companies, it is important to recognize that each sector has its own reputation features. You will be judged against others in your class and you need to know where you stand. For example, some sectors are reputationally challenged. If you work in the chemical industry, you are likely to have a lower reputational profile in comparison with other industries. However, it is important to know how you fare against other chemical companies, whether you have been able to separate yourself from the numerous reputational issues that attach to the whole sector.

The task is to work out, ideally with the help of your reputation consultative group, what are the big reputational drivers in your sector. For example, if you work for a utility, say, a water company, the big reputational issues could be 'sustainable use of water' and 'fair prices charged to customers'. I would recommend that you define a maximum of five key reputational drivers that are relevant to your sector in order to benchmark your reputational progress.

Brand reputation

Finally there is a need to establish what people think about your products and services. This is probably already well researched in your company. Most businesses have a considerable amount of research material on what their customers are looking for. PR people often need to do no more than look up the extension number of their company's head of research, call him or her, introduce themselves and raid the archives.

Again I would recommend that a maximum of five product or brand attributes are agreed on in order to assess reputation.

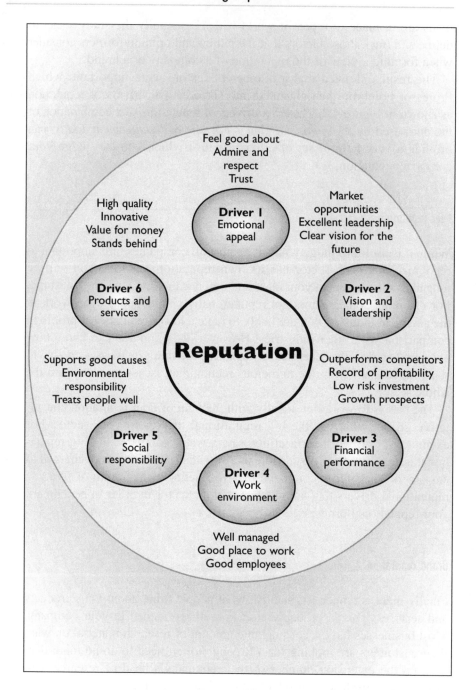

Feel good about
Admire and
respect
Trust

High quality
Innovative
Value for money
Stands behind

Market
opportunities
Excellent leadership
Clear vision for the
future

Driver 1
Emotional
appeal

Driver 6
Products and
services

Driver 2
Vision and
leadership

Reputation

Supports good causes
Environmental
responsibility
Treats people well

Outperforms competitors
Record of profitability
Low risk investment
Growth prospects

Driver 5
Social
responsibility

Driver 3
Financial
performance

Driver 4
Work
environment

Well managed
Good place to work
Good employees

Figure 4.2 Attributes and drivers of reputation

Source: Professor Charles Fombrun of the New York University Stern Business School

Taking corporate reputation, peer reputation and brand reputation together, it is then helpful to plot all of the key drivers on a single reputation scorecard, as shown in Table 4.3.

I would always suggest that a number of these reputation scorecards are developed, perhaps one for each key audience or for each key issue, major part of the business or a particular brand. Different audience groups will have different priorities and therefore you will need to tailor your messages accordingly.

The differing priorities between audience groups is vividly illustrated by the results of the research completed in the UK by the research firm MORI (Table 4.4), which provides a very helpful insight into the priority lists of different groups. Charts such as this can help PR people to create targeted campaigns that hit the sweet spot for any given audience, as opposed to reputationally bland campaigns that miss the main points for all concerned.

While separate reputation scorecards for each audience group are undoubtedly helpful, it is essential to create a single composite scorecard

Table 4.3 Reputation scorecard – example													
	−6	−5	−4	−3	−2	−1	0	1	2	3	4	5	6
Corporate reputation													
Emotional appeal													
Products and services													
Workplace environment													
Vision and leadership													
Social responsibility													
Financial performance													
Peer reputation													
Sustainable use of water													
Fair prices													
Brand reputation													
Innovative new products													
Committed to local economy													
Developing new markets													

Key: −6 = extremely poor, 0 = neutral and 6 = very positive

Table 4.4 Criteria for judging companies

Q: What are the most important factors you take into account when making a judgement about a company?

	General public	Politicians Lab (left wing)	Con (right wing)	Business press	Financial investors
	%	%	%	%	%
Quality of products/services	25	33	53	56	66
Customer service	21	53	33	38	33
Treatment of staff	20	70	14	21	16
Financial performance	15	25	56	94	90
Quality of management	12	38	32	94	88
Environmental responsibility	4	34	19	9	11
Social responsibility	2	40	17	12	11

Source: MORI

for the entire organization, in order to provide a single measure of reputation at a glance, as shown in Table 4.5. This example of a reputation scorecard shows the current score (marked by an X) and the desired score (marked by an O). This company is aiming to move its reputation score from 2.82 to 3.64.

You will see that there is a numerical scoring system for each reputation driver. Businesses like numbers; they like scores, ratings, indices and figures that can be tracked over time. My advice is that if you can express your reputation as a figure, you will be listened to within your organization. Activities that can be measured and quantified are respected and supported.

The aim should be to establish a set of reputation indices or scores. Even one index figure is better than none at all. These indices can be referred to over time and compared with the competitors. Just as people refer to the latest Dow Jones figure or the air temperature, so you too should look to establish a commonly understood reputation score for your organization that becomes part of the common corporate language.

The way to do this is to conduct research with your target audiences and ask them to score your business on a scale, say, –6 to 6, where –6 is where you are very negatively viewed in this area, 0 is a neutral or nonexistent profile and 6 is excellent. Respondents give a score against each reputation driver, and then do the same for at least two of your major competitors.

	−6	−5	−4	−3	−2	−1	0	1	2	3	4	5	6
Table 4.5 Reputation scorecard with stretch goals													
Corporate reputation													
Emotional appeal							·		X		O		
Products and services									XO				
Workplace environment									X	O			
Vision and leadership									X		O		
Social responsibility										XO			
Financial performance										XO			
Peer reputation													
Sustainable use of water										XO			
Fair prices								X		O			
Brand reputation													
Innovative new products								X				O	
Committed to local economy											XO		
Developing new markets									O		X		

Key: −6 = extremely poor, 0 = neutral and 6 = very positive
X = actual rating; 0 = target rating
Goal: to move reputation score from 2.82 to 3.64 in 18 months

You will then be able to plot your reputation and give yourself an average reputation score. This will tell you where you are now and what are your strengths and weaknesses. The next task is to set yourself reputation stretch goals. In other words, this is what your reputation is now, and this is what would you like it to be in, say, 18 months' time.

These targets are a very useful discipline and will help you to prioritize the PR activity for the coming years. As well as being vital in terms of informing the content of the PR programme, they can provide very effective targets which can be used to motivate yourself and your team. Some companies, for example, link bonus payments to movements in reputation scores and many organizations are increasingly linking an element of the fees paid to external PR consultants to the achievement of reputation score targets.

Traditional market research is the pure way to create such a scorecard and track it over time. However, this can be too expensive for many organizations, and there are alternatives. The first is to conduct the research virtually, that is, imagine the results that you would have if you did possess the budget to carry out external research. What score would you achieve if you asked your target audiences to rate you against the selected reputation drivers? This is an exercise you can complete on your own or preferably with the support of your reputation consultative group.

Another way of forming a view is to analyse what the media is saying about you and your competitors. How are you being portrayed in the print, broadcast and electronic (Internet) worlds? Is your coverage promoting your strengths in the key reputation areas? What is being said about you that is negative? You can then transfer these to a reputation scorecard.

The benefit of this is that media coverage can be evaluated at a far lower cost than conducting traditional market research. However, the downside is that it does not probe awareness among target audiences in a deep way that connects coverage with changes in attitudes and behaviour. For example, your media coverage may not report your expertise as a business that is involved in the community, and therefore you would secure a low score in this respect.

However, you may be engaged in significant direct communications with local community leaders, political figures and so on, rather than via the media. So, in fact, your level of awareness could be very high with the target audience but this is not reflected in the media coverage.

In other words, media evaluation alone, although very important, only focuses on output, when in fact what matters the most is outcome, that is, the behavioural shifts and actions of the target audience. When designing PR planning tools, it is always important to focus on the desired audience response rather than on the tactic of communication. There is no point achieving acres of media coverage about a new product if people still do not buy it. Similarly, it is not a measure of success that you have 20 meetings with politicians to explain your point of view, if these politicians do not then act on your appeals. In both cases, the PR team have 'done a lot', but clearly the content and approach were inappropriate, as the desired audience response did not take place.

So far we have looked at how to measure levels of favourability, in other words what people think of you and how they compare you to competitors. While favourability is clearly important, we need to look at familiarity and the importance of measuring the quantity of awareness and media coverage versus competitors.

Woody Allen said that the world is run by people who turn up. There is no doubt that the same applies to building a winning reputation. Those that have a high profile normally have a high favourability rating. Familiarity breeds favourability. If a senior business figure is always in the media talking about issues of the day, or a certain company is always in the public eye, there is no doubt that people generally have a better view of that individual or organization.

Clearly there are exceptions, for example crises, when businesses or individuals are in the media for the wrong reasons and this does not always give them a favourable reputation. However, in most cases, 'being there' will raise your favourability. Many companies feel satisfied with reputation scores that are neutral, but the truth is that a neutral score is another way of saying that you are invisible.

In addition, those organizations and individuals which are active in building their profile are assumed to be good companies in all the areas that are considered when audiences are contemplating reputation. If a company is generally seen to be high profile, contemporary and successful, we are more likely to assume that they are good employers or are heavily involved in helping communities, even though these are two areas where we are unlikely to have an informed view, unless we work for the company in question. This is the reputation multiplier effect, where those companies or individuals with a strong reputation and a high profile will often be credited with more than they genuinely deserve.

What is happening is that, by having a high and positive profile, those companies and individuals are building a trust bank account with us. They win trust credits by demonstrating that they are innovative or responsive to consumer needs. This convinces us that the organization or individual could be entrusted to take on new responsibilities. We believe in them. They have earned our confidence and therefore we can picture them acting in positive ways now and in the future. Such companies have built up a reputation fund which is based on potential reputation value.

These companies find that they are often approached for new projects, whether it is to be included on a new tender list, or develop a new aspect of their business or industry sector. Potential employees often put these companies to the top of their wish list with recruitment firms, financial analysts will often recommend the stock more readily, venture capitalists will be more likely to lend them money and so on. These organizations have built up a reputation force field which beams outwards, hypnotizing us all and winning over our support for the future.

The lesson is clear, you cannot build a winning reputation if you are corporately shy. You need to be in the media, in the public eye and a reputation management player on a regular basis. You need to keep the hubbub bubbling with editorial coverage, advertising, events, literature, direct mail; these all need to be employed to ensure that you are regularly on air and dominating the share of voice. Whatever you do, do something.

Audience prioritizing and role definition

The next step in building your reputation identikit is understanding the audiences that matter to your business. Typically, these will fall into two categories: friends and foes. Sometimes friends become foes and vice versa. Your job as the person in charge of developing a winning reputation is as follows:

- Define the audiences that matter
- Understand their current point of view – is it negative or positive?
- Think about what they are interested in – their priorities
- Think about why they are important to the organization and to you
- Consider how and to what extent they may be turned into friends and, once they are friends, how they can be enlisted and mobilized to help you to achieve your goals
- Consider the best way to reach the people that you need to connect with.

The first of these two points will be answered by the research that we have looked at. Finding out what their priorities are, what media they consume, how they source their information, how they operate, what sort of people they are and so on, can all be addressed by research.

However, less expensive and more immediate ways of familiarizing yourself with the target audience do exist. For example, if you are interested in reaching environmental groups, you should join their organizations, read their publications, attend their conferences, talk to them, in other words, do whatever you can to get an understanding of their psyche, priorities and modus operandi.

Understanding how your target audience thinks and operates is key to being able to appeal to them and present information in a way that will engage them and enlist their support. However, as well as understanding how they operate, it is important to know why they are important to you and what they can do either to damage or enhance your success. Often this is obvious, but on occasion it may be necessary to spend some time researching the external environment to establish how decisions are made, the influences involved and the role of each audience in shaping the agenda against which you operate.

Winning friends and winning reputations

The final step is to think about what you need to do to win over each audience group. In some cases, and with some issues, you will never succeed in winning over opponents. Strongly held religious or political views, for example, are never going to be overturned by PR, no matter how effective. There will often be hardline extremists or just people incredibly set in their ways who you will never win over. In which case, the strategy should be to isolate their views by ensuring that those with a more moderate outlook who come in contact with the extremists are already predisposed not to listen, or be influenced as much as they would have, if you had not set out your side of the argument. The main target of any PR campaign is almost always the open minded or floating voter. Thankfully, this group normally makes up the majority of society on any issue, so it is an audience worth pursing.

For those who can be won over, it may be that you need to build a sturdier case to convince them of your point of view. This might mean, for example, that you conduct some new research to support your arguments, stop using controversial business practices, or perhaps meet these people more often and thereby increase the level of communication compared to the past, in order to build trust and sympathy towards your position.

This systematic approach to bonding with your audiences will help to focus your priorities and efforts towards winning their support. This process is all about winning trust and almost always takes time and effort. It is a slow, often rocky road and not for the faint-hearted.

Winning over an audience has many stages and it is important to recognize that the relationship can get worse before it gets better. To help to illustrate the various stages that audience dialogue normally takes, I have developed the reputation ladder (Figure 4.3), and it is your job to move each target audience group up each rung.

First, to get people to put a foot on the bottom rung of the ladder, you need to attract their attention. A basic awareness that you, your business and its brands exist at all is the first task. Typically, mass communication techniques are most useful here. This is normally via the media, so advertising and editorial coverage are essential, although posters and direct mail all have a part to play at this stage.

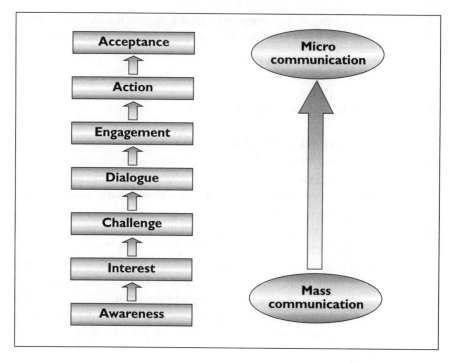

Figure 4.3 The reputation ladder

Once aware, the target audience should become interested, depending on how targeted and relevant your communications are. This is why total preparation is vital because you need to know what your target group is interested in and therefore what they will respond to most enthusiastically.

The next rung on the reputation ladder – challenge – is often the one that surprises and puts people off in the reputation management business. It is at this point that lesser reputation builders turn around and go home. The truth is that once you stick your head above the battlements, people will try and shoot it off.

However, believe it or not, this is a good sign. Naturally audiences start to ask questions once they are interested in something: does this new product really work? Isn't it very expensive? Why do you use that chemical in your products? Why should I come and work for you? And so on. Again preparation is key here. You should have anticipated every challenging question and thought of convincing, credible answers, with the facts to back them up.

Unlike justice, reputation is not blind and this is a critical time in the building of trust. How you answer these challenges will determine whether your audience moves up to the next rung on the reputation ladder, or whether you have lost their trust and your support slips down again. The advice I give to clients at this point is not to lose heart in the face of challenge, but be ready to respond and take on your critics in a firm and credible, yet sympathetic manner.

If you are successful in winning over their challenges, your audience will then move up to the next rung which is dialogue. When dialogue is happening you are in with a chance. When people are talking there is always hope. Your brand is being considered. It will be chosen if you can move your audience to the next stage – engagement.

With engagement, your target audience is working with you. They understand your point of view, their knowledge is now deeper and they see you as a player in the grand debate. They have everything they need to act (the next rung on the reputation ladder) and hopefully they will now respond and behave in a different way (a way that is more favourable to you and your business) than they would have done before you began communicating with them. In other words, they have moved from their current position to your desired position.

The final rung is the nirvana of reputation management – acceptance – where your brand, company or point of view is accepted as part of the everyday landscape. This could mean that your brand is now regularly purchased, that your company's viewpoint on a particular topic is always considered, or that your target audience now trusts and respects you and includes your position when considering its own.

As you move up the reputation ladder, generally it is the case that the nature of communication changes from mass communication at the early stages, to more intimate, micro communications, such as face-to-face meetings, personalized direct communications through print or email, or joint working and even strategic partnerships (the equivalent of a marriage in reputation terms). Examples of this are shown in Case Study 10.6 of Kraft Jacobs Suchard's partnership with Romanian health authorities and Case Study 10.4 of Unilever's work with the Turkish Ministry of Culture for its Cif clean-up campaign.

Stage 3: safe foundations

Having worked out what you want to say, who you want to say it to and how, you would have thought that the next logical thing to do would be to go out there and do it. Action is essential, of course, but before you go forth and spread your gospel, it is essential to carry out a full reputation risk assessment. Angels fear to tread until the crisis and issues management plan is set in tablets of stone. The fact is that issues will exist in your business which will hinder your plans to have a winning reputation. Issues are like rocks that people throw in front of you as you drive along. And if the issues are the rocks, the people throwing them are your opponents, such as competitors, pressure groups, anti-capitalists, elements of the media, unions, there may be many people against you.

Welcome to the world of issues management. Issues management is all about:

■ Identifying the risks to the business's reputation from the outside world and internal shortcomings

■ Being clear how probable and damaging these issues might be

■ Understanding what the business can do to remove or reduce the threat

■ Understanding who is interested in each issue and what damage or help they can provide

■ Being prepared to handle the issue if challenged.

Identifying the risks will require a combination of an analysis of the media and research, perhaps new work, or a desk research project looking at what is currently available. It will also benefit from an internal risk and communications audit to ask the business what reputation issues exist, what the business is already doing about them, which activities are working well and what still needs attention.

A typical risk and communications audit would consist of interviews, which should be conducted with:

■ Senior executives within your business, asking them what they think should be the communications priorities

■ Existing PR practitioners within the business, asking them what activities they are engaged in, what works well, areas for improvement, as well as finding out what skills are needed that are currently not available in the business

■ Any existing external PR advisors, in order to assess their role and perspective on the company's reputation management processes, for example areas of strength, weakness, threats and pockets of opportunity

■ The media and other external audience groups, to ask for views on the quality of the communications materials and contact they receive from the business – how helpful it is (or not) and what else they would like to receive or know about the organization that would be helpful to their own agendas.

I would always recommend developing a structured questionnaire to conduct the interviews. In some cases, this can be mailed to people for self-completion. However, face-to-face interviews are ideal, but even then it can be useful to have a written questionnaire to provide structure to the meeting. It can also be helpful to mail the questionnaire to respondents before the face-to-face interview to help them to gather their thoughts.

A typical communications audit will involve talking to between 20 and 50 people. Overall the aim should be to establish:

1. What communications activity is currently employed

2. What is working well and what needs improving

3. What core values and achievements of the business should be communicated externally

4. Who is doing what and where there are any skills gaps (if any)

5. What the communications risks are (where we could be caught out) and what the communications opportunities are (where and how we could improve our reputation profile)

6. What needs to be done to address the issues highlighted by the audit, including budget requirements and changes to business practices.

In addition to the audit, risk identification is another key area for the reputation consultative group. One technique is to ask each member of the group to score the issues facing the business, for example by allocating one hundred points across the top ten issues facing the business.

Not only does this oblige people to identify what matters to them, it can also be a very useful tool when it comes to deciding on resources. Once the priorities are set, you will be able to look at how resources are allocated and ensure that priorities and resources are matched according to the needs of the business overall.

It is essential that this risk identification procedure conducted with the reputation consultative group is repeated once a quarter to ensure that old issues are downgraded and new ones added. Issues are fashion items, one minute everyone is concerned about the work–life balance, next it is the environment and so on. The flavour of the month changes with the whims

of the media, the public and politicians, so it is vital that the issues identification process is refreshed at least quarterly, if not more frequently,
should you be involved in a fast-moving area such as retailing, politics or
food production, all of which have new issues almost daily.

Identifying the issues is one thing, prioritizing them is the next step. It is
important to remember that you are working to identify reputational
issues, not business issues, and there is often a great difference. For
example, one dead mouse found in a sandwich produced by a company
that makes millions and millions of sandwiches world-wide is not a big
business issue; however, it is likely to be a major reputation issue that will
catch the eye of the media and the public.

One useful technique is to score each issue identified as to whether it is
serious and whether it is probable. You can use a simple high, medium,
low grading system. Those risks that are identified as being serious and
probable, clearly need tagging as red, those probable but not serious need
to be tagged amber and those improbable and not serious need a green tag.
They all need managing, but by categorizing them in this way you will be
able to focus resources more effectively.

Once the issues have been identified, the next priority is to attach relevant audience groups to each issue, as described earlier. In other words,
which audience groups are important to each issue, what do they currently
think on the issue, what you would like them to think or do and how can
they be reached, influenced and motivated.

With the issues identified, and the target audiences lined up, the business then needs to prepare for battle. This is the reputation protection
stage, when a business needs to build up its fortifications to be able to
manage the onslaught once it chooses to leave the safety of the corporate
citadel and go forth into the world to claim new reputational territories and
branding high ground.

To be a leader you need to be able to face your critics and win them
over. Building a winning reputation demands that you protect your reputation as much as promoting it, and there are some key factors that must be
in place before you open your corporate mouth to speak.

First, you need to try and remove any negative issues if possible, in other
words, change the business practice which is causing you so much trouble.
If demonstrators are outside your factory every day because you are using a
certain ingredient or employing child labour, can you stop using the ingredient or the child labour? The most effective way to have good reputation is
to be a good corporate citizen, so be one as far as is possible. This is illustrated in Case Study 10.16 of the Paulicentro Hazardous Load Terminal,

where real changes to the business were just part of the communications-led transformation.

In addition, you will need to prepare your organization to handle difficult questions. This will involve developing question and answer (Q&A) documents that raise difficult questions and offer (hopefully) credible answers. These documents are for internal use only and can be very helpful in getting the organization to think about a specific issue, the risks, where it stands and what it has to say for itself.

Q&A documents are also useful single points of reference, where a great deal of essential information can be held in one place for easy access, for example if a journalist rings up. They need to be regularly updated, for instance if a new issue appears in the media, it should be incorporated in the master Q&A document in case it comes up again.

One of the shortcomings of Q&A documents is that they quickly become huge tomes. This brings two problems; first, they become unwieldy and difficult to use under pressure, and second, senior people talking on behalf of the company do not have time to read them and, even if they do, there is too much data to be remembered.

One technique to get around this is to develop a key issues statement brief. A key issues statement brief focuses on the two or three really tough questions behind an issue, which need credible responses. The thinking here is that these are the big questions that are likely to be raised and essential to get right, the rest is detail.

Media training your way out of trouble

Another vital part of preparing a corporation to manage issues is ensuring that you complete adequate media training. Media training is essentially rehearsing the way in which you will deliver your arguments to a challenging interrogator, whether it be a journalist, your workforce, a representative from a pressure group, a politician or an agitated consumer.

As well as helping to prepare yourself in terms of delivery, media training is a very helpful way of focusing the mind and refining key messages. It is also a useful way of testing whether answers sound credible and convincing. Often a line put together in the supportive environment of the boardroom ends up sounding like PR propaganda when said to a lay person such as a journalist. Media training provides a safe environment in which to hone responses that do not quite work out the first time around.

The process should be to write the key messages and Q&As before the media training, test them for robustness in the training, then refine and retrain the spokesperson until they sound believable. It is advisable to use an external media trainer. Although a strong in-house person can perform the role, it is often easier to use an external consultant who can be highly aggressive in their questioning. Also they are able to ask the naive questions that are posed in real life and which are often so disarming.

Typically, a media trainer will video you answering questions and this is very helpful to gain a sense of how believable and confident your answers are under pressure. It is also a very good tool to see the progress made; it is often striking how much an interviewee will improve from their first take to the next one, after media training coaching. And remember, in real life there is no second chance, so an investment in media training is well worthwhile.

Media trainers will have various techniques, but mainly they will ask you to focus on delivering clear, reassuring and concerned responses. When responding to any difficult question, it is essential to structure the answer into three key segments:

1. *Concern:* 'yes, I share your worries'

2. *Perspective:* 'but you know we make thousands of these every day and the vast majority of people like them'

3. *Action:* 'nevertheless this incident is very serious and I will do something about it'.

Another useful technique that can be developed and practised in media training sessions is question bridging. It is important to remember that most journalists or people in general will have given little thought to the questions that they ask you; their main concern will be to lure you into saying something which compromises your position or which forces you into making a confession.

Your role as a spokesperson is to build a bridge between the difficult question and your key messages. Your aim should be to give the same answer to every question or, to be more precise, rather than an answer, give the same set of key messages over and over again.

This is quite a difficult skill to acquire. Handled badly, the risk is that you are seen to be avoiding the difficult questions, at best this can annoy your questioner and at worst make you appear deceptive, thereby confirming the allegations which you are clearly choosing to avoid.

However, with practice and training, question bridging can be used to great effect to turn what is often a casual negative opening gambit into a platform to deliver positive points. An example might be:

Question: 'With the closure of this factory, your business must be on the edge of collapse?'

Answer: 'Closing this factory was a difficult decision and one we did not make lightly, but the key thing is that it will allow us to focus our resources on the highly successful areas of our business which are x, y and z, and that means we will be in a better position to create more jobs in the future.'

As can be seen, without appearing heartless, the answer has flipped the negative into a positive. This technique of question bridging is worth acquiring and any media trainer will help you to practise this effective reputation management skill. Once the technique is learned, it is possible to improve this skill yourself, by spending a little time preparing for the worst before every major reputation management meeting.

Another key point is to ensure that sufficient spokespeople are trained and briefed. First, you need to ensure that you are covered for holidays and people being away from the business, but also it is important to be able to offer a range of spokespeople to suit the audience. A government enquiry commission needs a senior figure, while a scientific journal requires a technical expert. A 25-year-old journalist from a women's magazine will relate better to a younger brand manager (ideally female) and an issue relating to employees will be best handled by a human resource expert.

Critically, make sure that they have all been put through their paces beforehand.

Crisis ahoy

A few words about crisis management. Issues management is really about crisis avoidance. It is a business process which is designed to head off crises. An issue is a threat to the business which rumbles along, but occasionally that issue can turn into a crisis, for example if a high profile individual is suddenly caught up in the issue or if the media or a pressure group suddenly decides to highlight the subject for whatever reason.

Good issues management will either avoid the crisis or will help to manage the crisis more effectively when it blows. This also applies to emergency crises, major traumatic incidents such as a factory explosion, serious train crash, death of an employee or customer. Well laid out contingency plans to respond to and manage crises of this magnitude will pay dividends but must be put in place before, not after, the crisis has occurred.

Professional and thorough issues management preparation can pour cold water on a smouldering crisis, preventing it from igniting into a full blown inferno. Two case studies illustrating this are FedEx (Case Study 10.5) and Bolivian Airlines (Case Study 10.15), where both organizations managed a crisis into a reputation enhancing opportunity. For example, if you have been quietly briefing opinion formers on an issue and telling them about what you are doing to address a problem, they will be in a strong position to defend you if a flustered journalist comes on the phone digging for dirt.

It can be very helpful if an authoritative opinion former – the sort of person that journalists go to for comments – can turn around and say: 'well actually this is not such a big story as you think, this company is doing a very good job, for example they are actively investing in addressing this problem area, so you are really barking up the wrong tree'.

A comment such as this can throw a journalist off the scent and turn a potential bad news day into nothing more than a bad hair day. On the other hand, if the opinion former is not briefed, they will be unprepared and possibly embarrassed. This often leads to people speculating without substance, which can inflame a situation.

If you want to take this area seriously, there are two golden rules for establishing effective crisis and issues management plans:

1. The worst will probably happen

2. Be prepared for the worst.

By assuming the worst and then preparing for it, you will be establishing the safe foundations needed in the reputation architecture blueprint. Without this stage of preparation, the reputation of the business will always be balancing on a pinhead.

Stage 4: structural strength

With good foundations in place, the challenge is now to build a PR edifice that can stand tall come rain or shine. The key here is to establish a winning combination of resources and processes to ensure that your carefully honed plans are delivered effectively.

Much of the work has already been completed, a feel for the quality of the company's PR skills (both within the organization and supplied by external consultants) will have been covered in the communications audit.

Reputation strengths and weaknesses also will have been identified. The task now is to put it all together as shown in Figure 4.4.

The task is to join up all the disparate elements into a cohesive programme. Figure 4.5 shows the full range of audience groups that you should be thinking about when drawing up a final work plan for the reputation management team. It provides a useful checklist of audiences and areas of reputation management which you should at least consider before going into battle, even though some will not be relevant to your organization.

Figure 4.5 should be viewed in conjunction with Figure 4.6, which shows the principal reputation tools and routes that should be blended together into a reputation management plan for feeding out to the major stakeholder groups and areas of reputational activity identified in Figure 4.5.

Your work plan should ensure every aspect of reputation management works together holistically.

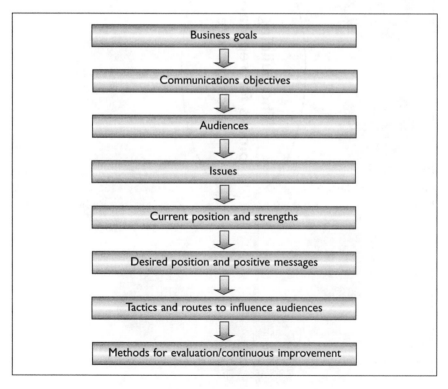

Figure 4.4 Joined up reputation flow

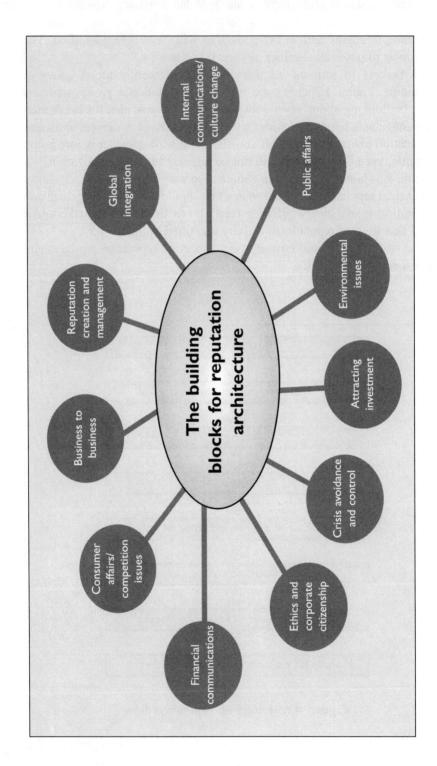

Figure 4.5 The audience/activity checker

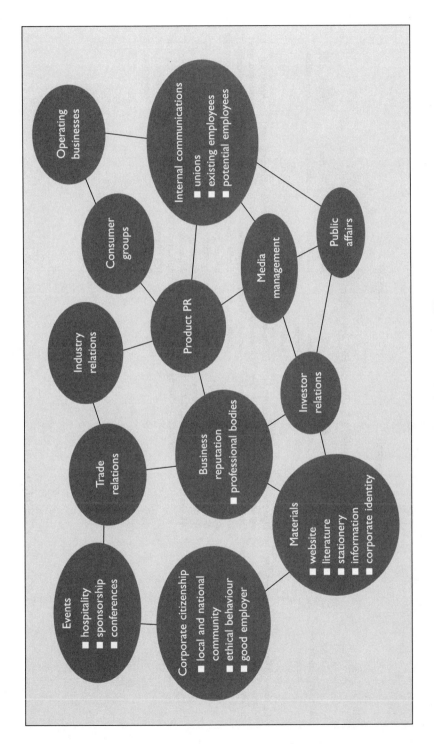

Figure 4.6 Joined up PR

Table 4.6 Typical PR work plan

Key message	Target audience	Current position	Desired position	Potential issues	Route to influence target audience	Required materials	Tactics for delivery	Method of evaluation
Bigstore creates quality jobs	Local politicians	Bigstore has created unemployment in small local towns and any new jobs created are low calibre	Bigstore offers high quality careers and attracts wealth and inward investment – overall it is a net job creator	Union opposition to job losses, low pay, senior management positions not held locally. Risk of planning permission refusal by local authorities	One-to-one meetings with local politicians conducted by senior vice president twice a year	Information on local jobs created in similar towns by our company. Introduce schools campaign to explain career opportunities of working at Bigstore	Meetings with politicians, schools campaign supported by media relations and in-store poster campaign	Research changed views of politicians, balanced media coverage, agreement by a minimum of three schools to accept visit by Bigstore representative

Once you have checked off the areas and audiences for attention, it will be necessary to put together a detailed work plan to manage reputation. Table 4.6 is an example of a typical work plan to address a fairly typical PR challenge. In this case it concerns a major retailer (Bigstore) looking to move into a new town and meeting with resistance. The chart shows how the issue will be tackled by the reputation management team. Clearly a considerable amount of detailed work underpins this plan, but it is nevertheless a useful exercise to sum up the task. Table 4.6 shows how just one message is delivered to one audience.

Clearly a typical business would have many such projects and several audiences to address and the PR team would need to lay each one out in this way on a master action plan, so that everyone is clear how professional reputation management is supporting the goals of the business.

Such a disciplined approach will win the support of colleagues and demonstrate that PR is a management discipline like any other, which can be planned and measured and not only add value, but also transform the very nature of a company and the individuals within it.

The rules of PR engagement

With the detailed plan in place, now is the time to set some ground rules for its delivery. Especially if professional reputation management is new to you and your business, you will certainly need to establish some reputation management protocols within your organization and within your own working day. For example, stipulating that only media-trained, authorized spokespeople should talk to external audiences. Or that all new advertising campaigns should be run past the PR team to check for any contentious issues. Similarly, you should look at how calls from the media are handled, what systems are in place for dealing with out of hours calls and so on.

The communications audit will have indicated which systems are working well and which are not serving the business properly. Now is the time to put in place all necessary improvements.

Intelligence gathering

Setting up a good media and external environment monitoring system is an essential process to have in place in order to track how the business is perceived, but also to monitor competitor and other relevant activity in the outside world.

The reputation management team should also now be setting up archiving processes to record details of PR campaigns that are successful so that they can be used throughout the organization or adapted for use elsewhere, for example in other markets or countries where the business operates. As an ongoing process, the company that is looking to build a winning reputation will be sharing good practice in PR and at all times encouraging the entire organization to use PR to its full effect.

Creativity is king

While process and planning in PR are vital, there is one other area that is just as important and that is creativity. At the end of the day, PR is about attracting attention and this means that you need to have creative techniques that stand out. Creativity is the extra element which brings a PR plan to life.

When thinking about things to do to make yourself be noticed, the key word to have in mind is 'relevant'. It is quite easy to think of stunts and initiatives that will attract attention, for example posing with a celebrity, or saying something completely outrageous. But will these help you to deliver your business goals and your communications message? Probably not.

Often what we want to communicate is not, in its naked state, that interesting to the outside world. That is why relevant creativity can lift a dull story into something noteworthy by dressing it up in alluring finery. A number of cases studies illustrate where this creative approach has turned lead into gold: Gestetner, the Eckard Corporation, Samsung and Post Oreo O are fine examples worth examining (Case Studies 10.1–10.3 and 10.8).

One of the keys to effective creativity in PR is to put yourself into the mind of your target audience and think about what appeals to them. A journalist will be looking for something newsworthy, not for simple information about your business, and therefore you need to present the information you want to deliver in a way that engages them and plays to their needs. The same applies to when you are talking to a politician, a consumer or an environmental charity for example. You need to think about their needs, their concerns and their agenda and deliver your message in a vehicle that will help to relieve their pressure points. The case studies of the Cif and Rama brands managed by Unilever and the ABS/CBN project are strong examples of companies tuning in to national, issue-based themes (Case Studies 10.4, 10.13 and 10.22 respectively).

Relevant creativity is about packaging your messages in a way that will appeal to the hot spots of your target audience and which will catch their eye among the thousands of other communications messages that are delivered to them every day.

Creativity is a big subject that deserves its own book. But in many ways it is common sense. It is common sense to look at examples of creative excitement in the world around you – newspapers, how meetings are run, how people interrelate to one another, how films, plays and novels grab your emotional attention – and then to think of how you can tailor your message in a similarly enticing way, so that it will be usable and desirable for your target audience.

If you want people to listen to you, you need to seize their attention, speak in their language, show them what is in it for them and entertain and impress them. Creative thinking at this early stage in your PR planning will deliver this magic combination for you and take your reputation plan to the world.

Stage 5: ongoing maintenance

The foundations are set, the building is up and working like a well-oiled reputation management machine. All that remains now in the process of building a reputation architecture is to put in place ways of evaluating and ensuring continuous improvement in the reputation management process.

There are three main elements to checking how things are progressing. The first is to track *delivery*, that is, is the reputation management team (or you as an individual reputation warrior) delivering the plan? Are you having meetings with journalists, politicians and so on? Are you creating the website, have you built trust with your stakeholder groups? Are you delivering good value for money to the business?

This can be measured quite readily if a detailed work plan is developed, either you have delivered the promised activity or not. Company satisfaction is also fairly easy to gauge as a result of having set up the reputation consultative group which includes senior representatives from across the business who will no doubt tell you quite unequivocally if they are not being well served.

The next level of measurement is *output*, that is, tracking the activities as they happen externally. For example, this can involve media evaluation, or tracking attendance at events.

Finally you need to track *outcome*, that is, the changes in behaviour and attitudes that occur as a result of the PR activity. This can involve audience research to track perceptions, but it can also include tracking of sales leads, share price, increase in visitors to stores, increased spending per head and so on.

The key to effective evaluation is effective planning. If you are clear about what you want to achieve and how you will measure that progress at the beginning of a programme, it is relatively straightforward to measure results. Unfortunately, far too many PR programmes are either never evaluated, or the evaluation is thought about at the end of the programme when there is a strong chance of disagreement over what it was that the campaign was setting out to achieve. Such disagreement can be avoided if everyone is crystal clear at the start of the campaign about the measurable objectives that everyone is working towards.

With good planning at the outset, evaluation at the end of the campaign is easily effected and can be used not only to gauge success, but also to inform new campaigns and ensure that continuous improvement is applied in reputation management, just as it is applied in all other aspects of management.

With all these stages of the reputation architecture blueprint followed through, you will have built the solid heart of a reputation management programme for yourself and your business. To help to consolidate understanding of this essential phase in the building of a winning reputation, the five key stages are summarized in Table 4.7. These simple logical steps underpin this vital core to any winning reputation. Much of it is common sense, although sadly it is not common practice. A great deal of it is instinct, but very few PR practitioners put everything together in this holistic way and even fewer have the bravery and vision to implement such a systematic and challenging programme.

For those individuals that do take this challenge seriously they will find that building a winning reputation for their business will enhance the value of the corporation and its brands. They will also find that their status within the organization is raised as they are seen to be managing one of the company's most valuable assets – its reputation.

The added bonus for you is that, along the way, you will also be enhancing one of your most valuable assts – your career and your personal and professional standing.

Table 4.7 The five stages of the reputation architecture blueprint

Stage	The process	The result	Timescale to complete
Stage 1 Surveying the terrain	▪ Interviews with board members and other senior executives ▪ Away-day with PR practitioners to define mission and procedures ▪ Forming of reputation consultative group of senior executives to drive reputation management throughout the business	A communications strategy that the entire business shapes and which supports business goals	3–4 weeks
Stage 2 Sketching the finished building	▪ External audience research ▪ Desk audit of existing research ▪ Communications audit of internal PR resource ▪ Review of media, legislative and competitive environment	A benchmark reputation index and a clear picture of the organization's reputation, its strengths, weaknesses and opportunities	2–3weeks
Stage 3 Safe foundations	▪ Focus groups with reputation consultative group to agree messages ▪ Testing of messages with target audiences	Distilled messages and priorities to protect and promote reputation	1 week
Stage 4 Structural strength	▪ Quarterly issues management review with ongoing Q&As ▪ Crisis avoidance scenario planning and exercises ▪ Media training ▪ Identifying and reaching opinion forming advocates ▪ Installing PR processes (for example PR Intranet) to ensure sharing of best practice and continuous improvement ▪ Creative themes developed in workshops to platform key messages	A road map linking objectives with audiences which allocates resources needed to tackle issues and deliver results	3–4 weeks
Stage 5 Ongoing maintenance	▪ External media evaluation versus competitive set ▪ External audience tracking ▪ Tracking of reputation index over time ▪ Linking reputation management activity to sales, share price and audience profile	Evidence of the extent to which audience attitudes and behaviour have been influenced	Ongoing
		Total time frame	9–12 weeks

CHAPTER 5

You are your PR: living out your reputation

The previous chapter looked at the reputation architecture blueprint for any successful campaign. By following that model, you will ensure that you cover all the bases in developing a thorough, professional programme of work in order to understand and improve your reputation.

However, PR is not all about process. It is essential to remember that PR is really about making your mark and creating an impact that helps you to achieve your goals. PR and reputation management are creative activities. Good PR people need to have strong strategic minds as well as a flair for publicity. They need to understand that a good plan without good creative ideas will never work. The PR flow charts may look like the instruction book for a NASA rocket and the evaluation system can be as sophisticated as you like, but if there are no ideas that are going to grab the headlines, the plan will just gather dust (along with your reputation).

There are many aspects to creativity in PR. In this chapter we will look at the two most important creative elements of your PR programme – you and what you say. One major difference in the PR world is the effectiveness of the person behind – or rather in front of – any campaign. For a business or an individual to stand out they need to build a personality for the media and others to latch on to. Companies that choose not to have a high profile spokesperson set themselves a difficult task when it comes to building their reputation.

Most of us find it difficult to relate to a faceless corporation, or to feel trust for a grey company spokesperson. Often when we think of companies or organizations that we admire, it is because that organization and its values have been crystallized by one individual who regularly represents the company. Their charisma and success, as well as the fact that they are regularly in the public eye, have a strange, positive effect on us. Because they are successful and always in the spotlight, we assume that their company and its products are successful and of a good quality. We assume that the amount of coverage they get in the media reflects the size and stature of their company and that their personal performance is impeccable.

Think of Bill Gates and Microsoft, Michael Dell and Dell computers, Jack Welch and General Electric; these are all companies that we consider to be excellent, a perception based on a reality which is dramatically amplified by the high profile of the CEOs. Their more faceless competitors are hardly known to us.

These are high profile examples, but this phenomenon of a significant personal profile raising the reputation share price of companies and individuals above competitors can work for you, regardless of what profession you are in or the size of your business or organization.

For example, in the business of PR consultancy, there are individual PR advisors and firms of consultants that have developed a high profile in PR media and the industry in general far exceeding their size and true status. Often when one looks up these high profile agencies, it is surprising to see that in fact they are often a fraction of the size of some of the major, but faceless, PR consultancies.

In reputation terms, these companies are punching above their weight and winning. They are included on pitch lists because they are famous rather than because of their size or even their business success. This is a great place to be and is probably the best example of excellent PR and reputation management truly adding business value. In virtually every case, the high profile has been achieved by an individual willing to apply themselves to building a reputation that puts them head and shoulders above their competitors, even though many of their competitors could eat them for breakfast.

The PR consultancy market is not unique in this regard. These reputationally turbo-charged companies and individuals exist in every walk of life. By clever management of their reputation they cast a long shadow, making themselves appear far larger than they really are.

This personal PR activity is the most powerful tool available to anyone who wants to be their own spin doctor and build a winning reputation. However, many people find it difficult, both personally and corporately. True, there are risks and issues connected with building a high, personal profile, such as:

- If the reputation of the company is linked to a person, what happens when that person leaves or retires?

- A strong, high profile leader can make other executives seem like second-class citizens to clients and colleagues; 'why am I not getting the top man?' customers often think if presented with another individual

▣ What happens if the individual falls from favour? Inevitably this will reflect badly on the company, as those that live by the reputation sword will die by it

▣ Shouldn't the brand or company be bigger than any one individual?

Each company needs to consider these risks and decide whether they build the profile of their leaders or simply aim to build the profile of the business and its brands. My personal view is that one should always go for building the brand and company profile by building up the profile of the leader of the business. Overall this has several advantages that outweigh the risks:

▣ Like it or not, public opinion of business, politics and most elements of public life is largely shaped by audience perceptions of the people that run these institutions. Performance is important, of course, but it is often not enough to win support

▣ The media and other opinion formers relate better to an individual with character than they do to a faceless entity

▣ Employees look to a strong leader to galvanize the culture and give a focus to the business

▣ Having interesting opinions and views does a great deal to build a reputation, as it requires a strong, brave character to express these views. It is difficult for a corporation to make attention-grabbing comments, but it is easier if those views can be pinned to and expressed by a single individual

▣ Expertise and acumen are more easily expressed by an individual speaking on behalf of a successful organization; credibility is enhanced if a person is willing to put their name to a statement or point of view

▣ It is human nature to relate to a person over a corporate entity. Those in the business of managing reputation should take advantage of this and build and promote to the outside world interesting people from within their business. If they appear successful and accomplished, these characteristics will be seen to apply to your business and its products.

For these reasons, you need to recognize that you and the other leaders in your organization are the best PR secret weapon that you possess. Even though it may go slightly against the grain, you need to get out there and strut your stuff. It is not vanity, it makes good business sense. You will boost the profile of your business at a fraction of the cost of traditional marketing. In addition, because you are using the third-party endorsement of PR, what you achieve will be real and deep rooted, something that is difficult to achieve through conventional advertising alone. You will also do your own personal career prospects no harm.

If you can master the art of personal PR promotion, you will soon find your business on tender lists alongside rivals twice your size. You will be noticed in your marketplace in a way that is far beyond the scale of your operation. Headhunters will be on the phone more often and your colleagues at work will begin to see you in a totally new light as a true leader and an excellent ambassador for the business, in other words, a serious player.

Becoming a micro celebrity

Let us now look in detail at how you can go about turning yourself into a big hitter in your field. The first thing to understand is that you need to be noticed by whoever matters to your well-being. Therefore, you need to appreciate that, like all celebrities, you are public property pretty much all of the time. Even as a micro celebrity (only famous in your own world), the same rules apply to you as to Tom Hanks or Kate Moss.

You need to recognize that, every minute of your working day, every where you go and with everyone you talk to, you are performing. Never let your guard down, you are always on duty. There is no such thing as an off-the-record PR moment. Phrases such as 'between you and me' and 'between these four walls' have no real meaning. You are always in a public mode of operation, even behind closed doors and among business friends.

How you look, how your office looks, what you say and do is part of your reputation management activity. Think about this before you make decisions about how you express your views, how you behave, what you wear, what you drive, what hobbies you have (or at least those you want to talk about) and so on. You are public property and public property needs public relations, so do not leave things to chance. Like any celebrity, you should look at nurturing your reputation as a meticulously planned activity. Chapter 6 looks in more detail at the physical appearance and stylistic aspects of reputation. But for now let us take a look at content – what we say and do to build a strong reputation.

This is after all the most important factor. While there are some celebrities who are simply famous for being famous, they are few and far between and are often despised for their superficiality. As a result, they rapidly disappear from the public gaze, never to be remembered again. One-hit wonders exist in PR as well, but what you should be aiming for is building real, sustainable interest in yourself as a professional for the long term.

Working out your key messages

The first stage is to think about and hone your script. In other words, you need to define your key messages. First, what are key messages? A great deal is talked about this and the need to stay 'on message' is a regular feature of business and political life. Unfortunately, this phrase is often narrowly interpreted, implying the need to toe the line and say only what is bland and acceptable. This is a type of self-imposed censorship and not really what key messages are about at all.

In fact, key messages are not about avoiding answering a question, they are more to do with being very clear about what you are trying to say, that is, reducing obscurity rather than spouting a smokescreen of propaganda.

Key message development is the art of taking the complex and boiling it down to easily understandable points that everyone can remember and instantly understand. Messaging is about working out the headlines that will make people remember your story. Case Study 10.7 about the Queensland Treasury Department is a good example of making a complex area easy to understand through the disciplined use of clear messages.

The process which I developed and used over the years to help myself and my clients work out their key messages is called 'message mapping'. Based on tried and tested presentation skills advice, message mapping uses the magic of the number three to deliver a point of view. Hence:

- Make your point/deliver your message

- Repeat it

- Then repeat it again.

Finding your 'master message'

The first stage in message mapping is to be clear about your 'master message'. This is the 'one big thing' you want to get across to your audience. You should be able to express it in a single sentence, ideally without any commas or phrases in parenthesis. When you write down your master message, try to keep the sentence simple and straightforward. Avoid conditional clauses or 'grey words', which reflect vague positions, thoughts and feelings.

To help to illustrate the point, let's pick a very simple master message to work through as an example. Let's assume that you are running a PR campaign to persuade business people to invest in your town. Your overall master message could be:

Your business will benefit if you set it up in Mytown.

This master message works because the language is simple, it appeals to the person receiving the message, because, rather than simply telling them how good you are, it tells the audience how they will benefit. The sentence is direct and like all good messages it whets the appetite. How can my business benefit? What is so special about Mytown? It is a message that intrigues and leads us on.

Sadly, such straight talking is rare in most PR communications. All too often impact is lost through overcomplication. For example, here is how *not* to express the above message:

For businesses looking to set up or expand, there are a considerable range of benefits available through special assistance schemes run by the Mytown Development Corporation, the country's foremost strategic location development partnership.

This is how to kill a master message – by burying it in a convoluted sentence, using grey words such as 'considerable', 'foremost' and 'strategic'. What you end up with is less of a master message and more of a message mess. The words used are not only grey, but they are overused business babble terms that flick a switch in the reader's mind to 'sleep'.

When you look at most corporate literature or listen to business people being interviewed, this type of windy (hot air) and windy (around the houses) language is what one normally comes across. Business people should take a leaf from the books of politicians who generally understand the need for clear messages, expressed in simple language and short sentences. Listen to the speeches of John F Kennedy or Winston Churchill and you will see what I mean. Typically their sentences were very short, their terminology was elegant, but couched in everyday language. Their chosen words were definitive and resolute.

The beauty of three – trident messages

Once you have your master message, you need to work out what I call the supporting 'trident messages'. The name comes about as there are always three points to be made – like the three-pronged spear, the trident. The trident messages support the master message by putting a little more flesh on the overall statement. So, continuing with our Mytown example, Figure 5.1 illustrates the point.

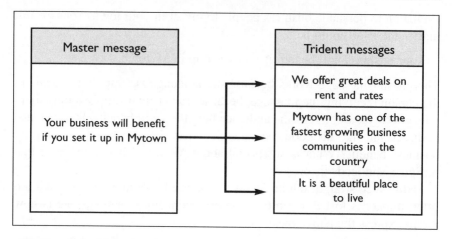

Figure 5.1 Message mapping: master messages and trident messages

Killer facts

The next feature you need for each trident message are some 'killer facts'. Killer facts are the nuggets of data that prove that the points of your trident are sharp and piercing – not just so much waffle and subjective claims. Ideally, killer facts should be simple statistics or vivid anecdotes. It is important to keep the numbers simple. Don't say: 'Between 28% and 32% of people, who over the last six to eight months visited Mytown, expressed a preference for Mytown over other similar locations.' This is accurate but far too much for the average brain to take in. Instead say: 'Around one in three people who visit Mytown say it is their favourite town in the area.' This is just as accurate, but much easier to remember.

Once again, let's return to our Mytown example and add the killer facts to the trident messages, as shown in Figure 5.2. As you can see, the killer facts are grouped against each trident message, with two killer facts per trident message. The purpose of this flow is to build a composite case, so that when you are delivering your message, each layer builds on the previous point to create a compelling argument. This is why you should seek to link each trident message together so that they supplement one another.

One way of doing this is to use the master message as a bridge between trident messages. Once the final trident message and supporting killer facts are stated, then the whole speech should be finally rounded off with a repeat of the master message for good measure.

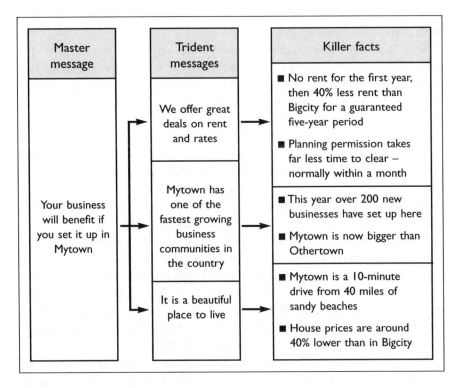

Figure 5.2 Message mapping: master messages,
trident messages and killer facts

So the flow might be like this:

- Mytown is the best place to be (master message)

- There are three main reasons why (trident messages)

- First, Mytown is the biggest – support with killer facts 1 and 2

- The second reason why Mytown is the best place to be (master message again acting as a bridge between trident messages) is because it is the widest – support with killer facts 1 and 2

- And the third reason (final trident message) is because it is the warmest – support with killer facts 1 and 2

- And these are the main reasons why Mytown is the place to be (end by repeating master message).

It can be very helpful to picture this way of thinking by presenting it in a flow chart as shown in Figure 5.3.

This technique should prove valuable in helping you to clarify the points you wish to make in a vivid and engaging way. When preparing this exercise, it might be helpful to imagine that you are suddenly face to face with a very important person in the lift, and, for the next 60 seconds, as you travel between floors, you need to get across your key points before the lift opens and you have lost their attention.

Think about such a situation and consider what you would say if you only had a minute or two. Are you prepared? Do you have all the facts at your fingertips? A few minutes of message mapping will be time well spent and will give you the quick-fire message delivery system that is necessary in a world where attention spans last seconds.

Message mapping can help you to manage a briefing with an important journalist, financial analyst, client or any key stakeholder. Every one of these stakeholders is busy and you will quickly find that, even if the meeting lasts an hour, their attention span is pretty short. They will only really be absorbing information for about 15–20% of the time that you are together. The rest of the time they will be being polite. You will need to convince them of your point of view pretty quickly.

A simple rule of thumb is that if they have not got your point within 60 seconds, you probably will have lost them. Not that they will necessarily leave the room, but their mind will probably be wandering.

Another important benefit of using message mapping is that it helps to improve the quality and sharpness of your thinking by testing your arguments in a decidedly rigorous manner. Next time you are preparing for an important presentation, sales pitch or media interview, try this exercise. First of all work out your message map, writing down master message, trident messages and killer facts, as well as working out the bridging technique that you will use to link each element together. Practise what you are going to say a few times on your own. Then ask yourself the following questions:

- Would a lay person understand what you have just said, for example if you explained it to your aunt at the weekend or to a friend in the bar, would they understand the points you are making?

- Does what you are saying sound believable?

- Does what you are saying sound distinctive compared to what has already been said by others on the subject before?

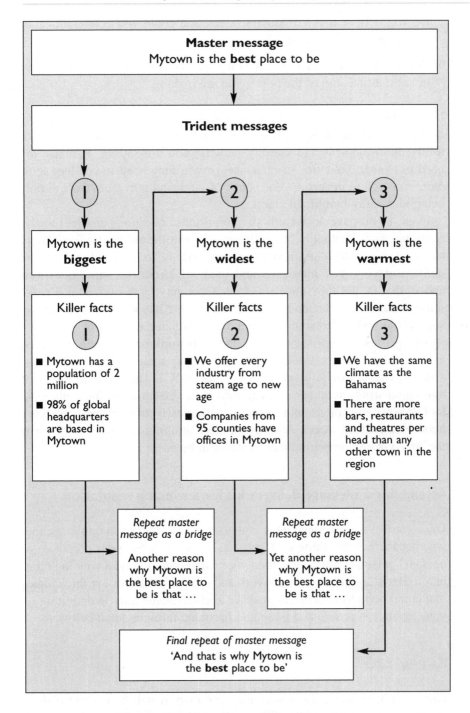

Figure 5.3 Message mapping flow chart

■ Do you believe in what you are saying and could you defend it against the toughest of questioning?

■ Would you always have a convincing answer if you were asked to prove or substantiate any of the points you are making?

If you answer 'no' to any of these questions, or even if you have any doubts, you are not adequately prepared and need to look again at the credibility, thoroughness and validity of what you are saying. Perhaps you need to change your line of response, or you may need to conduct some more research to underpin your points of view and turn them from simply being ideas into quantifiable facts.

Even if you have answered 'yes' to all these questions and feel totally ready for any eventuality, it is advisable to run the following final safety check. Ask a colleague, media trainer or friend to sit and listen to you delivering your key messages and then ask them the same questions above, that is, did they understand what you have just said? Did it make sense to them? Did it sound credible? Were there any weak spots and if so, what could you say to shore up your arguments in these cases?

This process of grilling yourself and your thinking will help you to be unassailably clear about what you are trying to achieve and the strengths and weaknesses of your arguments. Not only is this vital in terms of building a strong reputation, it can also be an essential business planning tool. If you can express your business ideas clearly, they are probably very good ideas. Clear speech flows from clear thinking and clear thinking is the strategic engine behind most successful business plans.

Assembling a message delivery kit for a winning reputation

Once you have determined what you want to say, it is worth thinking about whether there is anything else you can do to flesh out your corporate or personal persona before launching your campaign to build a winning reputation. Back-up facts, pro bono work and special initiatives are three topics that could be helpful projects in order to chisel some muscle definition on your reputation profile and these are discussed in more detail below.

Back-up facts

Once you have worked out your message map, it will be evident if there are any gaps that you need to fill in order to have a convincing story to tell.

For example, you may find that you need a few more killer facts, or you may need to collate a sprinkling of attention-grabbing anecdotes and stunning examples to make you sound genuinely persuasive.

If this is the case, it is important to put in place some activity to fill these reputation gaps, because at the moment these represent weaknesses in your arguments and that is always a dangerous place to remain. As mentioned earlier, in order to build up featherweight killer facts into heavyweight champions you could look at commissioning some new, supportive research. The case studies from Pharmacia Upjohn and the Hungarian National Health Protection Institute show how PR-led research can bring a campaign to life (Case Studies 10.18 and 10.19). This sounds expensive but it need not be. Here are a few tips on finding facts without spending a fortune:

- Pay a visit to your company's research team, the chances are that they already have what you need

- Contact your local college and see if you can pay a student to carry out some telephone or online research which will be far cheaper than commissioning a research company and, as long as the brief is clear, there is no reason why the quality should not be excellent. In addition, you will be giving a student some valuable experience and a little extra pocket money

- Send out a simple self-completion questionnaire to customers, staff or whatever group you are canvassing. This can be done very simply using email or via the post at virtually no cost. If you send enough out, you will receive a quite sizeable quantity of useful data. Expect a 2% response rate, therefore send out a sufficient number to ensure that you get a sensible quantity back in return. Remember to keep the questionnaire as simple and short as possible, that way people are more likely to complete it

- Do some simple desk analysis yourself of available literature, which could be trade publications, your own company documentation or publicly available materials from a business library or the Web.

These are just a few of the low or no cost ways that you can gather data. Clearly, commissioning professional research help brings added credibility and will often be necessary. The key is to ask the right questions and look for the appropriate data in order to defend your point of view. Start from your message map in order to discover what you need to know in order to prove your point.

Imagine that you are a lawyer building a case for a defendant: What is your overall defence and closing argument? And therefore what evidence and witnesses do you need to gather to ensure that your defence will convince a jury? The courtroom analogy is a useful way of preparing your thoughts and back-up materials. Put yourself in the witness box for a moment and then go out and get the evidence you will need to convince stakeholder audiences (the jury) that your story is worth listening to and is the correct version of events.

At the end of the day, the commercial jury votes either with their wallets, their votes or their views, and if you fail to convince them that your brand or company should receive their support, then you and your business will be leaving the courtroom as a loser.

One final golden rule about gathering data for PR purposes is to remember that this is information required to help make a PR point. It is not data designed to tell you something that you do not know, that is called market research. PR research and market research are two very different things and should not be confused. Market research tells you what is happening; PR research helps you tell people what is happening.

Pro bono work

This is where you or your organization take on work which is unpaid, but which will provide you with a reputation dividend in kind. Typically, this will involve you or your business supporting charity work, although this is not always the only route. An alternative example of pro bono work that is not charitable would, for example, be getting involved with a prominent and prestigious event, perhaps providing free goods and services at an industry awards ceremony.

Another non-charity-related example might be to provide employment to a notable person (such as a writer or a sportsperson), even where there is no immediate commercial need. Many companies have famous individuals on their payroll to help enhance the corporate folklore of that business.

The goal of any strategically relevant pro bono work in developing a clear and compelling PR persona is that it should provide you with something interesting to talk about. Also it can get you in front of some significant people. For example, if you are handling, without charge, a high profile court case or the launch of a new book or film, or working with a major charitable initiative, this will bring you into contact with a wide range of influential characters. In addition, you can add the experience to the credentials of your organization and to your personal CV.

Given that you will be working for free, it is clearly essential to select the most appropriate and useful beneficiary of your expertise. When selecting a pro bono cause to support, you should consider the following:

- Will my involvement put me into contact with my target audience?

- Does this pro bono work enhance my corporate reputation and if so how?

- What is involved – are the parameters clear and will I or my organization be able to fulfil its promises?

- Is the nature of the pro bono work strategically relevant and helpful to the goals of my business or my personal career plans?

- Will this activity be high profile and interesting enough to be a useful case study for my business and for myself?

- Is there a clear end point to this commitment?

These are wise questions to ask yourself before committing to any type of unpaid work. It is easy to be philanthropic, but you may as well be philanthropic *and* obtain some benefit for your business and yourself in the process. That way you are achieving a win–win situation, a win for the good cause or the recipient of the pro bono work, and a win for yourself. When both sides benefit, there is more likely to be a sense of value and the partnership will stand more chance of flourishing and having a long-term future.

Creating special units or initiatives

Another way of building reputational muscle is to commission a new activity that will put you on the map and back up your views with some action. For example, if your message map requires you to be seen as a leading thinker in the area of customer service, why not set up a special unit within your organization dedicated to innovation in this area. This will have two benefits. First, it will lend credibility to your claims about being a leader in this field; and, second (and probably most importantly), it will help you genuinely to be a leader in the field!

The best reputation springs forth from reality and this often requires you to make changes in the way you operate by putting money behind your mouth. Also, creating a new initiative, such as a special task force or a new programme, is in itself newsworthy and provides the media and other stakeholders with a focal point for your messages. It will also provide a PR occasion to justify your call to audiences to take an interest in you. It is a peg on which you can hang your coat of many messages. It is a conversation opener that stops listeners in their tracks. In addition, it will give your employees something to focus on and bring your innovation to the attention of senior personnel within your organization.

Engendering a campaign feel can concentrate effort and achieve great results. This can be especially true when any initiative has a clear launch and end point. This helps to demonstrate real progress over the campaign period, as opposed to having an open-ended drive for change, which soon flips into cruise control and PR oblivion.

Branding your new initiative – giving it a name and even a logo (as in Case Study 10.9 about Ljubljana University) – can also help to blow a bubble of enthusiasm that allows your campaign to float above the humdrum. Another option is to create a special Intranet or Web page. In addition, you could create a new job title for yourself or someone else in your team, for example 'Head of Project X', or 'Project X Development Director'. This will be very helpful when it comes to cutting through to busy journalists, political targets, opinion formers or even consumers. If the job title looks credible, the person will be seen to be credible. We accept job titles as shorthand credential statements. The right job title gives you permission to speak and, until you disabuse people, it adorns you with the believability and trust which is so critical in any PR and reputation building activity.

All these techniques will lend weight to the initiative and raise its profile and stature. However, the most important thing is that the innovation itself is interesting and really adds something that was absent before, both to the PR storyboard, but, most importantly, to the business itself.

A personal winning reputation plan you can stick to

Now you have defined the content of what you want to say and have a clear idea of who you want to say it to – courtesy of audience mapping – the next stage is to write a personal PR action plan and stick to it! Most people are happy to plan, scheme and daydream, but few are willing to actually do something about it. This applies as much to PR as every other walk of life.

The choice is yours: you can be a PR wannabe or a PR action hero. The advice is simple – get on with it. Building a winning reputation should be

10% planning and 90% doing. PR procrastinators never get anywhere. Take the decision to act. To have a winning reputation you must be a winner and you will never win the reputation race if you don't participate.

One way to ensure you deliver on your PR plan is to develop a simple winning reputation action checklist and timetable. Stick it on your office wall, look at it every day and then don't let yourself down. Complete every action, so no one can accuse you of having been all hot air.

Table 5.1 is a very simple example of a PR action plan, again using the Mytown example. Remember to keep your goals simple and your PR dreams will come true. To recap, the message map is as follows:

The Mytown master message is:

'Your business will benefit if you set it up in Mytown'

The trident messages are:

'We offer great deals on rent and rates'
'Mytown has one of the fastest growing business communities in the country'
'It is a beautiful place to live'

The killer facts are:

- No rent for the first year, then 40% less rent than Bigcity for a guaranteed five-year period

- Planning permission takes far less time to clear – normally within a month

- This year over 200 new businesses have set up here

- Mytown is now bigger than Othertown

- Mytown is a 10-minute drive from 40 miles of sandy beaches

- House prices are around 40% lower than in Bigcity.

Given this, the PR action plan for the Mytown project would be as shown in Table 5.1. This PR action plan shows how virtually every element can be linked to build up into an exceedingly active and cost-effective programme. Throughout the plan there are examples of where each section can be networked together to cultivate a superior force for communication. If only every PR practitioner developed a simple action plan and then simply delivered it, the PR world would be a better place.

Table 5.1 PR action plan for Mytown

Audience/ activity	PR action	Timing	Measurement of success criteria	Comments
All	Conduct survey on how successful businesses are that move to Mytown	Complete within 3 months	PR-usable data	Use local business school students to provide research
Media	Have lunch/meetings with two journalists per month	Over next 6 months	Twelve meetings completed – relationships established	In addition, pitch at least two stories per month to journalists
Opinion formers	Hold two drinks receptions for opinion formers, send written communication no less than four times this year & meet three opinion formers every month	Over next 12 months	Contact levels maintained – raised awareness as shown in tracking research	Develop opinion former newsletter to ensure regular communication vehicle
Top customers	Invite key contacts to breakfast meetings – aim to hold two meetings this quarter	Over next 3 months	At least 10 key contacts to attend each event	Find guest speakers for each event to cover relevant topic for our business
Trade associations	Join three main groups and attend at least one committee meeting every quarter	Over next 12 months	Attendance at events	Use topics covered as basis for editorial coverage in trade press. Include in opinion former newsletter and at one breakfast briefing event
Pro bono work	Select charitable cause to support by next summer	Within next 6 months	Suitable partner found and have agreed a relevant assignment with them	Invite high profile speaker from chosen charity to be guest of honour at breakfast briefing
Employees	Introduce quarterly staff newsletter and set up accompanying Intranet site. Establish special task force team to develop one innovation project	Over next 6 months	First report produced by task force in time for half year annual results	Ask HR department to include PR-related questions in annual staff survey to check levels of awareness of new PR campaign
Key suppliers	Hold three hospitality events	Over next 12 months	Annual customer satisfaction survey to check on improvements to supply chain management	Ensure at least one event is themed to reflect work of innovation task force
Politicians	Have one meeting with each key political contact and send regular opinion former newsletter	Over next 12 months	Include in annual opinion former survey	Invite political contacts to pro bono launch event
Recruitment consultants/ headhunters	Have two briefings for recruitment firms to ensure understanding of our business – send regular update letters to headhunters (min of three this year)	Over next 12 months	Conduct interview with all new joiners to check on how recruitment professionals are selling the company to prospective candidates	Print new introductory literature on company culture for potential recruits to help recruitment firms present our business

Table 5.1 cont'd

Audience/ activity	PR action	Timing	Measurement of success criteria	Comments
Business schools	Submit one case study every other month	Over next 12 months	Inclusion of our work in courses as examples of best practice	Invite business school professors to breakfast briefing events
Conferences	Meet four conference organizers and secure three speaking engagements	Over next 12 months	Attendance at events	Decide on three themes to speak on and commission new research as needed

You now have all the basics in place to go out and tell your story in a compelling, credible and high profile way. And remember, once you have your messages worked out, stick with them. It is better to give the same speech 20 times than a different one for every occasion. In addition to clarity, the other key for memorable reputation building is frequency of message delivery – saying it over and over and over again. And guess what? If you say something often enough, people believe it.

CHAPTER 6

Reputation as performance art

It ain't what you say it's the way that you say it, it ain't what you do it's the way that you do it – that's what gets results.

It is a truth, universally acknowledged, that only 7% of the impact we make on people is shaped by the content of what we say, whereas 93% of the impression we make is determined by a mixture of body language and appearance (55%) and the remainder by the sound of our voice (38%). Sound and vision matter more than patter.

While it is undeniably the case that you need to build a winning reputation from within, it is also a fact that living out your reputation in the way you speak, look and behave is the final link in the reputation supply chain.

Having looked at developing noteworthy content in previous chapters, I now want to cover ways in which you can build on that effort and make an even bigger impact in the minds of your audience.

While building a reputation is largely a rational process involving careful planning, application and determination, the full value of all that exertion will not be realized if you do not present yourself with flair and style.

Slick presentation skills will not compensate for lack of substance, but careful promotion of your messages will help you to persuade and win over support. Earning a winning reputation is a very human endeavour. As you are seeking to conquer hearts and minds, rational arguments will not be sufficient to secure both body parts. People need to feel motivated, inspired and willing to support you and this is greatly influenced by how you come across as a person.

You are far more likely to persuade if people like what they see as well as what they hear. Many business people or politicians are excellently equipped for the job, yet fail to capture the public imagination due to their lacklustre style or their unappealing manner.

Some individuals are born with this charisma and have a natural power to communicate in a mesmerizing way, but such people are extremely rare. For the vast majority of us, we need to think consciously about how we present ourselves and work hard to use our personal presence to maximum effect.

This is not to do with vanity, it is more a matter of not selling yourself short. You have decided to build a winning reputation and you deserve to have it. You have worked diligently to determine what you are willing to do to create that favourable profile and now you owe it to yourself to put your best foot forward as you take your reputation out into the world. By spending time thinking about how to present yourself, you will be giving yourself the best chance of seeing the benefits of all the planning and strategic thinking that goes on behind the scenes. Now is the time to get out on stage and be a star.

Working backwards to reputation

The eye sees not itself
But by reflection, by some other things.

(*Julius Caesar*, by William Shakespeare)

As the Bard correctly points out, our reputation exists in the mind's eye of others. How we see our own reputation is a kaleidoscopic reflection of other people's views and opinions as expressed in the media, people's purchasing behaviour and their attitudes as revealed in opinion research.

The best way to be memorable is to start at the end point. Consider the impression that you want to make and work out the things that you need to say and do in order to reach that result. Imagine how you want to be seen, how you want your business to look, how your offices should appear, what your literature should be like, how you want to be thought of and what the overall feel should be of your corporate and personal reputation. Once you have this vision in your mind, it is easier to lay out the stepping stones that you will need to traverse on the journey forward.

Sound bites – speaking in headlines

We have already looked at creating memorable messages backed up with killer facts. We have looked at the need to pepper your speech with these nuggets, in order to convey your points in a memorable way that simplifies and makes your point of view stick like a barbed arrow.

This technique of developing catch phrases and epigrams is a vital communications skill. Look up some of the phrases coined by masters such as Oscar Wilde or Winston Churchill and try developing some of your own. Even a complex theory can capture people's imagination if it is summed up in a memorable phrase.

Look around you for inspiration in newspapers, films, political speeches, plays, advertising slogans, song lyrics. Learn how others put together snappy headlines and memorable lines, think about your own business and the messages that you want to convey and then build a bridge between what you see and what you say. Spend that time in the bath or sitting on the train to concoct those killer lines to go with your killer facts.

Reach out when you speak out

Once you have your lines, you need to work on delivering them. Whether you are talking in public or addressing an audience of one across the table, think about the structure of your delivery. Bear in mind the key present-ation skills advice – tell them what you are going to say, say it, then tell them what you have just said. Imagine you are a journalist writing up the story you are about to deliver – what will be the headline, the body copy and the final paragraph? Or picture yourself as a lawyer in the court room and go through your opening address, the presentation of evidence and finally your closing speech.

As with message mapping, construct your presentation in such a way that you begin at the beginning and end at the beginning. Start with your main point, set out your rationale and return to your main point to seal the argument and steal the audience.

Punctuate what you say with your memorable lines, but also with pauses in all the right places. You can create a sense of drama and pace in your delivery by using silence to stress points. Pauses also give your audi-ence a chance to catch their breath and absorb what you are saying. Remember that people can only generally take in a very small amount of information at a single sitting.

Try not to speak too quickly or bombard your audience with too many concepts to keep in their mind at any one time. Around 130 words per minute is a pleasant rate to listen to and is the speed we are most used to from TV and radio. It will feel considerably slower than everyday speech, but when you are addressing a group it sounds perfectly acceptable from the audience's point of view.

Clear signposting in your presentation is also essential. These are occasional, simple cues that you give to your audience so they can be mentally prepared and to ensure that they are always on the same page of narrative as yourself. An example of a simple signpost would be to say: 'I want to talk about three key things' and then, as you progress, remind people which point you are on 'My first point is …', then later, 'the second point is …' and so on.

This sounds a very obvious statement to make, but, like many simple techniques, this verbal signposting is rarely used. Think of the times when you have listened to a speech and then afterwards have been unable to remember the vast majority of the points being made. This is a common occurrence, but clear signposting, a distinct beginning, middle and an end (which in fact is the beginning restated), as well as some memorable headlines and epigrams will ensure that your message is understood and remembered.

Tone and posture are the two other elements to work on when talking in public, even if your audience is only one person. Enthusiasm and energy are infectious and if you can display this in your language and style you will sound more credible and persuasive. So aim to inject musicality and variety of tone into your voice. Use aural light and shade to reflect the content. Also spend some time thinking about how you stand or sit and the extent to which you use movement to emphasize a point.

The essential rule is that posture and movement should underline and emphasize what you are saying rather than distract from your presence. So do stand firmly planted in a strong pose, but do not become so immobile that you appear wooden. Do use confident hand gestures to stress a point, but do not fidget or perform contrived, repetitive moves that become a distraction and betray your nervousness and hesitation.

As with media training, presentation skills can be dramatically enhanced by working with professional trainers in this field. Using video and role playing, they can help you to be aware of your physical presence and learn how to bring out your strengths. This power is within us all. You do not need to be a supermodel to create a stunning impression. Take Danny de Vito and Kevin Spacey, two men who, in the cold light of day, are not particularly physically appealing. They are not especially tall or handsome, they could pass you in the street as regular Joes. Yet both men have immense physical presence and charisma. They have a strong sense of self-confidence and a controlled yet natural way of conducting themselves that grips people's attention.

True, they have immense natural talent, but even these superstars benefit from talented directors to coach them and bring out the best they can offer. The same applies to people in business looking to build a winning reputation. A good presentation skills advisor will bring out the best in you by building on your natural talents, not by turning you into a fake performing seal. The best trainers take what is there and make it work even harder.

Whether you prepare with a presentation trainer or not, you should aim to turn your presentations into memorable pieces of theatre. Always strive to tell stories that inform, entertain and entrance your audience. When we are enjoying ourselves in a presentation, we absorb information and are more likely to be in agreement with the performers on the stage. Reputation management – like all business life – needs the skills of show business as much as it needs strategic analysis and PR craft skills. Your audience will always have limited time and attention and it is essential that you understand the most effective way to capture that brief initial period when they are receptive to listening and learning.

Top props

There are many physical signals that you can use to epitomize your reputation. These are the corporal and tangible manifestations of your reputational spirit, your personal character and values. For example, your clothes, the look of your office, your leisure pursuits, the restaurants you eat in, where you live, the car you drive, the films you watch, the books you read (or at least those that you have on your bookshelf), the plays you see, your hairstyle are all statements about who you are and what you represent.

If your desired reputation is to be reliable and traditional, everything around you in terms of appearance and lifestyle should support that positioning. Alternatively, if you wish to be seen as contemporary, not only do you need to look connected and in touch, but you need to be of the moment as well. This means designing a lifestyle that will reflect that persona.

Keeping in touch with the contemporary world is a professional duty for anyone interested in maintaining a positive reputation. Being seen to be connected to the modern world is an essential part of building a positive reputation that relates to modern audiences. In order to do this, it is important to be constantly refreshing yourself and your business to keep up with the times and to be seen to be keeping up with the times.

So, visit new restaurants, go and see new films and plays, visit different places, take an interest in our changing world and tune in to the zeitgeist. How can you influence current thinking if you do not know what current thinking is? How can you convince others that you have a viable and credible view of recent events, if your appearance, behaviour and frame of reference appears outdated and out of touch?

Here are a few of the key areas where you need to ensure that your reputation aspirations reflect your behaviour and style:

- *Clothes:* The right costume transforms every actor. The key here is to dress appropriately for the way you want to be seen. You should always buy the best quality you can afford, even if you have fewer items. Ensure that your look is contemporary by looking at magazines and checking that what you are wearing is what most other people are wearing. Regular culling of your wardrobe every three years will ensure that you keep reasonably up to date. Decide on a look that you feel is how you would like to be seen and then stick to the pursuit of that image. Dressing consistently is an easier way to make an impression than constant changes and experimentation. As with key messages, it is better to make the same statement 20 times, than it is to make 20 different points every time you are interviewed. The same rule applies to your appearance.

- *Hair:* As with clothes, you should check at least every three years that your hairstyle is similar to most other people's you see in the street. It doesn't matter if you do not like the look of the day, you should adapt it to suit your style and age and go with it. If you are in the reputation business (and we all are), you need to look *à la mode*, not outmoded.

- *Car:* This needs careful thought, but the process is pretty straight-forward. Ask yourself – if your reputation was a car, what car would it be? Then go out and buy that car. That is, of course, unless your desired reputation indicates that in fact you should buy a motor bike, or always be seen to take public transport. Consider what people would expect of you and your reputation and then live up to their expectations.

- *Office:* Your building and personal office space should be a reflection of your corporate persona. Reputations are credible when every element adds up to form a consistent, total reputation picture. If you claim you are an open, contemporary company, you need offices that are open and contemporary. Your corporate style needs to be reflected in your furniture, décor, material on the walls and the overall appearance and layout of your working environment. In addition, the physical work space itself is a canvas to portray your reputation. If your organization values innovation, you should display examples around the business. If your reputation goal is to be seen as excellent in a certain field, you should adorn the office walls with framed examples that demonstrate your achievements in that area. Similarly, your own office should be decked out in a style that reflects your values and priorities and provides you with props and conversation pieces that build the corporate legend.

▪ *Materials:* It can be effective to develop tangible materials that help to communicate your reputation. This is partly about ensuring that all the details work to complete the total picture. For example, business cards, the type of crockery in which you serve coffee, the style of the flower display in reception – all these small details should fit the desired reputation being built. Nothing should jar or be accidental. Everything plays its part and therefore should be planned.

In addition to these props, you could consider developing other materials to help to make your reputational points. For example, simple credit card-style items printed with your main messages can be given to all staff. Small leaflets are very effective for explaining the company's goals or its mission in life. Wall signs, posters, standard presentation slides and corporate background documents are all useful tools to help you to explain the DNA of your organization. In addition, they allow for others to tell your corporate story in a consistent way as they provide a set of tools that any representative can follow. Consider putting together a brief page of words that sums up your overall purpose which can be referred to by all. An excellent example of this technique is the Lord's Prayer, a single, short prayer that encapsulates the core values of a Christian life. Even if we can only remember this one item, we are a long way to grasping the basic messages of this religious brand.

▪ *Leisure activities:* as a micro celebrity, you are never off duty. Your choice of leisure activities will be a statement about your credibility as a contemporary leader. But perhaps most importantly, you should develop leisure activities that can feed your business's need to stay fresh and in touch with the world in which you operate. Everyone is entitled to some time off, but perhaps you could be using that time in a more fulfilling way that would lead to business, as well as personal, benefits.

Surprise others by surprising yourself

Pursuing leisure activities that are deliberately different to those you have done before is one way in which you can choose to rejuvenate your outlook on life and as a result your performance at work. Instead of always doing the same things, week in, week out, deliberately try to vary your behaviour patterns. For example, once a month, buy a different magazine to the one you normally buy. Choose something aimed at a totally different target audience than yourself. Go to a part of town that you have never visited before, watch a type of movie that you normally would not consider, watch a TV show that you have never even heard of. These are all simple ways of surprising yourself and learning about other worlds – worlds in which you are trading.

As well as keeping in touch, such enforced variety keeps you mentally fit by presenting you with new and alternative visual impressions and concepts. You should try to learn from these and build this experience into your work as a reputation builder. For example, what lessons can be learned in terms of creativity? Are there any new potential partners you have encountered, for example for joint promotional activity? All this experimentation keeps you fresh, but it will also ensure that you appear to be a current thinker, in touch with the pulse of society, which is essential if you are in the business of reputation creation and protection.

The grand gesture

Another way to be remembered is to make a few grand gestures. This could be a public commitment to stop using a certain ingredient in your product, a pledge to reduce queues in your stores, or a decision to buy every member of staff a Porsche. Whatever you do should reinforce your business culture and aspirations and not a forced stunt. However, a grand gesture often can underline a serious business message in a dramatic and forceful way.

The grand gesture also provides the basis for corporate anecdotes. These are an essential part of building a personal profile and a corporate personality. It is natural to relay tales and fables as examples of what a person or a business is like, but would be contrived to create these anecdotes artificially. However, if you think about putting in place an activity to epitomize and bring to life your reputation, then the anecdotes and legends will write themselves in the collective minds of your employees and the media. If you are going to act, you may as well act with flair and panache, turning a process into a performance that then goes down into the myths and legends of your micro celebrity and the reputation of your business.

Symbols

Another effective way to build a tangible embodiment of your conceptual reputation is to consider the creation of symbols that represent your values and ethos. One example might be pieces of specially commissioned art for your offices that reflect the spirit of your organization. Another might be a charitable scheme that you set up or support, that also reinforces your desired perception among stakeholders.

You may even consider a logo for your reputation – a sign that becomes a shorthand symbol for your values. Alternatively, your reputation symbolism could show itself in the form of a company policy. Fifty per cent of employees should be from ethnic minorities, no more car parking spaces for company directors, free private health insurance for every employee, meeting rooms without chairs to ensure lively discussion and brevity, a commitment to no animal testing – all these are examples of symbols that your organization can adopt to bolster a reputational stance.

The strongest reputations are built from the inside out. Flashy clothes, sharp haircuts and clever catch phrases are never going to be a sustainable alternative to real self-development and far-reaching improvements in corporate behaviour. However, once you have made the decision to have a winning reputation, part of attaining that prize is down to how effectively you communicate. This chapter has looked at some simple techniques which can help you to put forward your reputation with vigour. They are not about turning you and your business into something they are not. Quite the opposite, this is all about taking the spirit of your reputation and making it come alive in everything you say, in how you appear and behave.

A major element in shaping how your business is seen will be how you are seen. As a leader, you are your business. You represent the reputation of your organization and it is essential that you live up to that expectation in everything you are and do.

The areas we have covered in this chapter will help you to complete the full picture for those who are scanning the barcode of your reputation and checking that all the claims fit with reality. If your stakeholders are convinced that perception is also reality, you will have reached a significant milestone on the road towards establishing a sustainable and winning reputation.

CHAPTER 7

What the reputation consultants say ... and don't say

You might have been forgiven for thinking that as people spend more time working on understanding and improving their own reputation and that of their businesses, they might need less outside help from PR consultants.

As companies are recognizing that reputation matters and that PR sells, they are hiring more in-house PR professionals and building up departments of trained PR people. Today it is quite normal to have an in-house PR team of four or five people working full time in a major corporation at local company level and even more at the global or regional head office.

Some PR and communications departments have as many as 40 people, consisting of press officers working 24/7, investor relations teams, public affairs specialists, environmental experts, community relations advisors, technical writers, internal communications experts and so on, working to protect and promote reputation. Teams exist at a local level, within regional structures, covering brands and corporate reputation in a complex and often contradictory web of PR people and communications experts, all talking and listening on behalf of an organization.

Yet, with such a proliferation of PR practitioners, you may be surprised to hear that there has been no decline in the use of the external PR consultant by corporations, charities and governments.

In the past, the external consultant provided his black, mysterious art to companies who did not understand how the process worked. Today's in-house PR person is a total professional, often coming from a PR consultancy themselves. They understand the discipline, often know the journalists, politicians and other key contacts better than any external agency and they certainly understand the business better than any third-party consultant advisor ever could.

Despite this, rather than consultants being used less frequently, in fact quite the opposite is happening. The external PR consultant is alive and well and particularly thriving. Expanding in-house PR expertise has not ousted the external PR advisor. In reality, the external PR consultancy market continues to grow dramatically. Just ten years ago, the top PR consultancy in the UK was billing around £5 million worth of fees. Today the UK's number one is pulling in closer to £30 million in fees.

Globally, PR consultancy is building at similar levels in developed markets as well as in emerging regions. Established markets and their powerful economies drive the PR industry, as an aggressive media and intense competition push companies to ensure that their reputation is protected and their voice is heard.

The globalization of the media, and the scrutiny of the goldfish bowl that companies find themselves operating in, demands ever-higher levels of PR management. New developments, such as the Internet, the growing power of nongovernmental organizations, increasing consumer power and shortages of skilled labour, all are logs on the fire that stokes the PR consultancy furnace.

In an increasingly complex world, the reputational challenges multiply accordingly. The media is an insatiable monster, stakeholders want answers, information, views and comments all the time on every conceivable topic. Pressure groups demand responses, the financial community wants results, employees want more empowerment, information and personal satisfaction, charities want help, communities want involvement, and politicians want concessions, contributions and vote-winning solutions.

The load swells incessantly. The reputation business has turned into a hungry monster whose appetite feeds on itself – the more its gets, the more it wants. In-house teams mushroom in size in an effort to respond, but often achieve little more than standing still.

And, as in-house teams get closer and closer to their businesses, they often lose that sense of external perspective that drives the reputation agenda. After all, your reputation exists in the minds of other people. A business needs to think as others see it and, for the in-house team who become embedded in the corporate culture, this ability to view things from a distance becomes harder and harder.

Also, how can even the biggest and best in-house team keep up with the latest developments in the PR scene world-wide? How can they learn from others, how can they keep up to date in such a highly fragmented PR world?

The answer is that they cannot do everything and this is where the external PR consultants come into their own. The consultancy business offers another view and, for many in business, it is this external second opinion that is invaluable. It is a view that can resolve internal dispute, tip the balance in debates and act as a voice of conscience, caution and encouragement.

And it is not just in the developed markets that the PR consultancy industry is burgeoning. New economies too are realizing the benefits of communicating with audiences, selling ideas and opening up company cultures, which once were controlled, closed or nonexistent.

The privatization and liberalization of whole country economies, as well as industry sectors such as utilities and transport, have driven the need to adapt and keep a competitive edge within a changing environment. In addition, governments increasingly use external consultancies to help them to win elections, or mount public awareness campaigns around health issues, educational campaigns and other projects for social change.

Charities, too, have increased their use of external advisors, as have trade associations, trade unions, schools, universities, research centres, hospitals, business schools, campaign groups, publishers, and pressure groups. Case Study 10.11 on the charity Lions Club International is an excellent example of how this sector is benefiting from the professional application of external PR advisors. It is now commonplace for businesses and organizations routinely to use external advisors to help them to get their points across.

This interest in reputation feeds on itself. The more that people take reputation seriously, the more the task's true scale unfolds. Those companies that decide to take an earnest approach to building a winning reputation, setting up an experienced in-house team and hiring an external consultancy, in fact find that the PR workload increases rather than decreases.

The process of applying a more systematic approach to PR and reputation management reveals areas of significance that previously were neglected. These can manifest themselves as audiences that were missed or skeletons in cupboards needing a proper burial. Also, the more you communicate, the more audiences appreciate this service. Like Oliver Twist, they return for more, tell their colleagues and expectation levels around information provision rises and rises.

All this commitment takes time and resources. Often people hire a consultancy in the hope that it will lead them to spending fewer hours on PR work. Almost always – and especially if the PR consultant is doing a good job – the time spent on PR increases as the discipline is treated more seriously.

External PR consultancies look like they are here to stay and will continue to thrive for some time to come. At the end of the day, their popularity with businesses, individuals and organizations is that they provide an external viewpoint which, by definition, cannot be found from within, so the existence of consultants is likely to be a permanent feature.

Getting best value from PR consultants

The role of the external counsellor is one that has helped kings, CEOs and companies throughout the ages. It is a service that is as needed today as ever. So how should you go about selecting and using an external advisor? How do you get the most from them? When can they add value and when do they not? These are not easy questions to answer and many people become frustrated by the service that they receive from external PR consultants.

Some people have long and fruitful relationships with their external PR consultancies and advisors. However, all too often, client retention by PR agencies is poor, with many accounts not lasting beyond the make or break three-year period that seems to be a watershed for relationships between agency and client.

All too often, it seems that year one is the settling-in period, with an added honeymoon factor. Year two sees the cold light of day cast over the relationship as both parties begin to grasp each others' strengths and weaknesses and define how client and consultancy will work with each other, hopefully to add value. Year three is then either the final straw, or the happy consolidation of all the teething problems and learning, leading to a real foundation for a powerful alliance.

Of course all this can be blown off course by changes at the consultancy end, which is highly likely, given that average agency staff turnover is typically between 30% and 50%. Or, equally disruptive, changes occur at the client end as new brooms sweep in and sweep out the old, in favour of the new. This often takes the form of employing an agency used in a previous job, so it is not so much 'out with the old, in with the new', but more 'out with the old and in with a different old that I know from the past to be my sort of consultancy'.

While most consultancies do have some long-standing clients, the truth is that, generally, client retention records are not something that many consultancies can boast about.

Many smaller, often individual, consultants do possess client relationships that go back decades. However, as in advertising, familiarity tends to breed contempt and clients are frequently keen to chop and change in their search for the 'miracle PR cure', which they feel has got to be waiting for them at another consultancy.

But is all this promiscuity a good idea? Do clients really get a better deal by agency hopping? Is there truly a magic PR bullet out there with their name on it? Or could they get more out of what they have already got? And if so, how should they go about getting best value and best results?

The obvious starting point is to be clear about why you need an external PR advisor and what you want them to do for you. Although this seems obvious, it is a constant source of amazement to external PR consultants the world over as to how little their clients think about why they have an outside PR resource.

What the agency does, its brief, its role as part of the in-house team, its strengths and where it adds value are often ill defined. When the role of the external advisors is so unclear, for the client and for the advisors, the prospects of long-term success are slim.

Therefore, the first step in getting the most from an agency is to know precisely how they will help you to reach your goals. This presupposes one key element, which is that you are clear about your own PR goals in the first place. In previous chapters, we have seen how to create a PR plan for oneself or an organization, so by now it should be relatively easy to develop a clear strategy and programme of activity in order to help you to build the winning reputation that you want and deserve.

Sometimes it can be useful to involve external PR teams in this development phase, rather than waiting to involve them after the plan is done and dusted. External PR experts can help you to develop a full PR plan that perhaps takes into account areas which you have not even considered. Often PR people can help to point out those facets of reputation which you may miss.

They can help to supply thinking and resources, and sharpen PR objectives by providing a context and a sense of perspective to ensure that the goals are achievable and useful. Often they have specialist knowledge of audience groups, or expertise in specific areas such as internal communications, corporate social responsibility, environmental issues, regulatory affairs, or niche media skills such as in the interactive or broadcast areas.

Securing your external consultant to help to develop your overall PR plan can be a useful way of winning their full support when it comes to implementation. This will result from having been closer to the plan's conception, but also from encouraging them to sign up to methods of evaluation against which their performance can be judged.

It is also far more motivating for external PR advisors if they believe in the overall goals of the programme and feel that they have had a hand in shaping them. Similarly, it will be far more motivating if they have jointly agreed the key performance indicators that will be used to judge the success of the PR campaign and their own contribution as external advisors.

When to turn within and when to turn without

Once the overall plan is agreed and clear, the next stage is to review the existing in-house resource and assess where, if anywhere, there may be a skills or experience gap that could prohibit the overall success of the plan. The following are typical areas of skills and experience required to develop and execute a modern, sophisticated reputation management programme:

- Writing skills
- Understanding of the use of photography
- Literature production
- Understanding of broadcast media
- Understanding of interactive media
- Understanding of print media
- Creation of audience lists and databases
- Development of evaluation processes
- Creativity skills
- Strategic planning skills
- International PR management expertise
- Crisis management
- Issues management
- Public affairs knowledge
- Financial community communications experience
- Corporate social responsibility
- Media training
- Intelligence gathering
- Preparation of positioning statements
- Experience of working with celebrities
- Managing opinion former contact networks

- Developing links with trade associations and other relevant nongovernment groups

- Speech writing and conference planning

- Video production and editing

- Strategic consultancy.

These are most, but not all, of the skills that could typically be required in a PR department. The next task is to consider which of these are essential or only occasionally desirable, and then decide whether these skills already exist or whether they can be best acquired by training of in-house personnel, recruitment or through the retention of an external consultant.

Typically, the use of external consultants will be preferable to recruitment or training of in-house teams in the following circumstances:

1. The skill is highly personal to an individual or an agency and is not easily transferable, for example a sector knowledge, a technical understanding of a certain area, or a specific grasp of an issue

2. When the skill or requirement is only needed for a relatively short period of time, for example during a crisis or for a peak of activity such as a major product launch, or an event

3. When the in-house team have neither the time nor the mindset to achieve results in a certain area, for example generating creative ideas or the development of a specific campaign that otherwise would get put to the bottom of the in-tray if it were just another task for the in-house team

4. When the cost of transferring the skill would be prohibitive, for example it may be that to hire someone with a level of expertise such as that possessed by the external consultant is beyond the resources of the business

5. When there is a recruitment freeze in an organization, yet funding still exists for external support on a temporary basis

6. Where the type of experience required needs specialist and expensive equipment

7. When it would take a considerable time to develop such a skill within the business.

Occasions where it is suitable to develop skills in-house rather than hire an external consultant could include:

1. Activities which require a high level of involvement, enough to warrant a full-time post and where rapid and constant access to the business is required. A good example here would be the press office function

2. Skills which are easily learnt or readily available, such as media skills, copywriting, or event management

3. Where a considerable degree of co-ordination of reputation and communications management is required, for example across company departments or geographic regions. This will require an individual to network actively within an organization and create links and connections – a role that is typically hard for an external person to secure

4. Tasks that are frequently carried out and which are capable of being managed as simple processes. There is rarely any need to pay high consultancy rates for basic PR tasks, even if they are essential functions of the PR team.

Having assessed the gaps in your in-house resource which you will not be meeting from your own business, the task of defining the contribution that will be made by external consultancies is far clearer.

Extracting the most from your dream consultant

The first task is to find the right consultant. Typically, most companies hold 'beauty parades'. This involves a list of between six and eight agencies or individuals presenting credentials, in order to create a shortlist of three or four agencies. Normally those shortlisted are asked to prepare detailed, fully worked out proposals. The company then selects one agency as the overall winner.

The whole process is time consuming and requires a substantial amount of work and expense for the consultancies involved. The company taking the pitches will also experience a great deal of management time being absorbed by this process. The timescales can be protracted – a month from initial credentials to final appointment would be remarkably fast – two or three months is more typical. Inevitably, ongoing PR work goes into abeyance during the pitch process. Then there will be at least another month of PR downtime while the new agency finds its feet.

Changing and selecting external PR advisors is an undertaking which should not be taken lightly. Clearly it is a very important decision as your PR advisors will be intimately involved in your business on a daily basis. They will be hatching and cradling one of your organization's most precious assets – its reputation. Your career prospects also will be at stake, as your PR advisors will be seen as your representatives within an organization. They are the face of your business, your department and yourself so how they perform reflects on your own feats as a reputation manager. If they fail, you will get the blame, not the consultancy.

In addition, you are likely to be paying a fairly large amount of money for your external advisors. Although modest when compared to management consultants, lawyers and advertising budgets, it will, nevertheless, represent a significant investment. Demonstrating and gaining value for money should, therefore, be a priority.

Given all these important factors, once the consultancy has been selected, how well do businesses use this significant investment? How effective is the 'beauty parade' in picking the best people for the job? How effective is it – given the disruption – for companies to change their advisors like people change their socks? Or are the biggest dividends paid on the longest term investment – do those that stick with their advisors, beyond the first hint of dissatisfaction, actually get a better deal in the long run?

Client surveys show a mixed picture; however, most indicate a steady improvement in overall client satisfaction levels over time. This could well be due to investments made by the PR consultancy industry in professionalizing itself, through training, investment in technology and the adaptation of quality improvement processes and reputation management models based on best practice.

Consultancies have also invested in new and specialist areas where they can achieve economies of scale. These specialist pockets of expertise would be very costly for an individual organization to develop, but a consultancy can spread this cost across several clients and offer these specialist services and individual leading gurus at a reasonable cost and to a very high standard.

The fact that the consultancy market has been growing so rapidly must indicate that overall satisfaction levels are strong and improving. PR advisors report a move towards clients using their services more discerningly by focusing on areas where the consultancy has a discernible skill that the client organization lacks. So consultancies are providing fewer commodity services and instead are moving steadily up the corporate chain, increasingly reporting directly to CEOs or to director or senior vice president level communications chiefs.

The consultants' advice on consultants

So companies are using consultancies more than ever before, but are they getting the most from the transaction? How can you get a better deal? Perhaps the best way for an organization to find out how to get the most from their advisors would be to ask them what works well and what does not. What do the consultants themselves make of the people that hire them?

However, there is one flaw in this – how do you know that your advisor will tell you honestly what he or she thinks of the relationship and how effective is the service being provided? Many external advisors would find such a discussion welcome, but perhaps difficult, given that it may well involve questioning the value of both their own service and the value that their current activity provides to the business.

While this reticence is understandable, it is regrettable, as there is no doubt that PR consultants could teach us all a great deal about what makes a great PR campaign and what does not. Over the years they will have seen many examples of companies and individuals toiling away at managing their reputations. They will have seen it all and that awareness and knowledge of good and bad practice could be very helpful if it was shared without fear.

It was for this reason that I decided to conduct some research for this book among external PR professionals to see if they could share their observations of what makes a great PR campaign and also to harvest their views on the most effective ways to use an external PR team to best effect. Based on their collective years of experience of working with clients of all shapes and sizes, what have they observed as good practice in terms of turning a winning partnership between PR consultancy and client into a winning reputation?

Anonymity was essential for the survey. Although most practitioners were happy to be named, few wished to cite specific past and present clients, except when the reference was positive. And indeed there were many positive references to clients, indicating that the external PR advisor and client experience had a two-way flow of benefits in many cases, with PR advisors being happy to acknowledge where they had learned from their clients. The best relationships were mutually beneficial and a self-developing experience for both parties.

The survey acted as a type of confession box for PR advisors, who could come in, be hidden by the grille of anonymity that a self-completion questionnaire offers, and yet still talk openly about the daily waste they see in their work with clients. More constructively, they were able to share their views on the characteristics of those clients and campaigns that were effective and which truly benefited from close working relationships with their advisors and agencies.

In all, 32 PR advisors gave up their time to participate in the survey. They came from a wide range of organizations: from single PR counsellors to those working in major, international PR firms. As you might expect from PR people, who, by definition, are likely to be first-rate, active communicators, the responses were expansive, colourful and frank, but always with a positive outlook and a plea for clients to listen and learn from their advice and experiences.

In fact, the research showed that 'the client who is decisive' seems to be the one who achieves the most from the consultancy relationship. When asked what made a good client, the ability to act with determination came out as the highest factor (Table 7.1).

Clearly a client who is committed to working with an advisor as a partner and a colleague is a key element within the successful formula. But this needs to be coupled with a passion for action and a desire to apply PR enthusiastically and with vigour.

Perhaps it seems strange that this needs to be expressed as a criteria, given that PR is all about communicating and standing out in a positive way. However, one of the most common complaints from PR advisors is that clients lack the bravery and bias for action that effective reputation building requires. Faint heart never won fair lady – and it will never secure you a winning reputation.

As has been stressed already, to have a reputation that is interesting, you actually have to be interesting. Speed is also important. Media deadlines wait for no man and often the first to speak out sets the tone. First mover advantage applies in PR as much as it does in every other area of business. All too often, PR consultants see the ossification of corporate spirit as a result of business leaders' crippling conservatism, self-doubt and fear. The

Table 7.1 The consultants' view: what makes a good client?

	%
Is brave, has a clear vision and takes a strong lead/acts quickly	69
Sees relationship with PR advisor as a long-term partnership	41
Listens and takes advice	31
Has good/realistic understanding of what PR can achieve	25
Pays on time and adequately	19
Is grateful for advice and help	12

result may be safety, but the company, its people and its character remain invisible, overlooked and unfulfilled.

So if bravery and a commitment to a long-term partnership of PR adventure are the ingredients for success, do these results always improve if clients use the same PR advisor over a period of time? Not necessarily, was the answer the consultants gave. According to the survey, an over-whelming 84% of consultants felt that the most powerful results were achieved when there was a long-term relationship with the agency as a whole, coupled with partial changes to the team from time to time to keep things fresh. 'Familiarity can dent performance' was how one consultant described the risks of never changing the team line-up.

While it was observed that the best results often came from refreshing the team, it was also noted that a long-term commitment to the agency and the programme of work usually paid dividends. There was strong recognition that reputations take time to create and images cannot be painted overnight. 'We do the impossible at once, but miracles take a little longer', quipped one PR advisor in the survey.

Perhaps this is one of the most surprising and useful pieces of insight thrown up by this survey. On the one hand, we have virtually all the PR advisors saying that they see the best results occurring when there are well-managed changes in the account team. On the other hand, clients feel that the time spent in building knowledge of their business is wasted and they become irritated by the need to rebrief new team members.

While some continuity is clearly desirable, and while it is also the case that agencies could probably do more to ensure that knowledge is trans-ferred effectively to new team members, could it be that clients are actu-ally losing out by insisting on consistency of teams?

Surely companies risk losing one of the key factors that an external PR advisor brings – the fresh viewpoint of someone outside the business. Clients are too often like dominant partners in a marriage: attracted at first by differences, contrasts and complementary characteristics that drive them to win the hand of their consultancy. However, once hitched, they seek to dominate and suppress the consultancy's differences and fresh viewpoint. Indeed, they seek to create replicas of themselves. Like dogs and their owners, consultants and clients often end up looking alike. They can rein-force each other's views rather than challenge and stimulate debate.

While this can sometimes help – being on the same wavelength can speed decisions and smooth the path to finding solutions – all too often it leads to inactivity and complacency, as consultants slowly 'go native'.

The best results from consultants, according to the research, seem to come when there is a bedrock of knowledge about a client's business, but when, despite this, the advisor still sees the client through a child's eyes, or at least through the eyes of the outside world. That way the consultant can keep on challenging, asking those naive questions and translating the corporate message into a language that the outside world will comprehend. One of the best ways of achieving this is team changes, yet it is a technique that is largely despised by the very people who will benefit from it most – the clients.

One radical action for a client to undertake – based on the insight that this survey of consultants reveals – would be actively to encourage and plan for team changes. So, instead of fearing and avoiding change, perhaps clients should act like soccer managers and occasionally replace a tired team player with a newly picked substitute who will bound onto the field with fresh energy.

What makes a great PR guru?

Let us imagine that you as a client have decided to take on board the advice outlined in this survey of PR advisors. You pledge to listen to your consultant's advice, act on it decisively and commit to a long-term partnership that you keep fresh through regular new team line-ups. Once you have decided to be a paragon client, the next thing is to find a consultant to match, who deserves to be part of your reputation building programme.

But how do you spot a good one? This question was put to the advisors themselves in the survey. After all, they have had more experience of PR consultants than most. Over the years they will have worked alongside dozens of consultants – good, bad, sloppy and terrific.

So what makes a great consultant? What qualities do they see, day in, day out, as the ones that deliver results for clients? What sort of person makes a superb PR counsellor and therefore what should the client look for when selecting a PR partner for life?

The results were fascinating for several reasons. First, there was relatively little consensus. Unlike other questions, respondents gave a wide range of characteristics to describe a typically first-rate PR advisor.

The second interesting revelation was that the most frequently cited qualities were essentially human characteristics, more to do with personality and character than specific PR craft skills. Again this contrasts sharply with many clients' requirements, which seem to focus more on hard-core credentials rather than an overall flair for the job.

Admittedly clients also look for a strong 'chemistry fit' between agency and client, but they seem to place more weight on factors such as relevant sector experience and personal contacts, than do the consultants themselves when considering what makes for an excellent external advisor. It is worth remembering that skills and contacts tend to be largely transferable commodities, whereas personality and character are unique to an individual consultant. Clients might, therefore, be better off if they looked beyond the skills and contacts to the person behind the credentials (Table 7.2).

Hopefully, this survey of observations from PR consultants on how to get the best from an external advisor will help those looking for a new advisor. But it should be just as useful to those who feel they would like to derive greater value from their current consultancy team, if only they knew how.

The fact is that it is only in an anonymous survey such as this that you are likely to hear the truth. In the end, PR consultants are in business and their advice will be determined by whatever helps them to prosper. Normally this is not an issue, as the self-balancing forces of the market mean that client business will naturally gravitate to where value is delivered. And value is likely to be delivered where the consultancy is deriving profitable, sustainable benefit from its clients. As in all business life, a win–win situation between client and consultancy delivers the most effective results in the long term.

But it is clear that, to get the most from an advisor, you must treat them like human beings (because they are). Listen and act on their advice. Get

Table 7.2 What makes a great PR guru?

The PR consultants' view: what are the most important qualities for a great PR consultant?	%
Ability to listen	25
Resilience	22
Ability to communicate clearly	19
Curiosity	12
Common sense	9
Lateral thinking	9
Integrity	9

Other qualities mentioned by less than 5% of respondents:

Diplomacy
Flexibility
A strategic mind
Antennae
The ability to translate ideas between communities

what you pay for – advice. But remember, not only do you get what you pay for, you also end up paying for what you save, so it makes sense to keep budgets at realistic levels to ensure willing support, partnership and a complete service.

When it works, the relationship between client and external PR advisor can be an intimate and crucial part of building a winning reputation for yourself and your organization. A good advisor can build your career, develop your company's business through profile building, change corporate cultures and transform the fortunes of yourself and your organization.

Alternatively, they can burn budgets and deliver apparently nothing. The outcome lies in your hands. Hopefully, the results of this research will help you to make the right choices with confidence and enjoy the rush of working with cutting-edge, professional PR practitioners.

CHAPTER 8

The new e-economy: what it means for those building a winning reputation

Ever since the Industrial Revolution in the late eighteenth century, there have been new technologies that have changed the way we operate and exist as people. It is a natural human conceit to assume that, whatever the latest development may be, it is the last word in sophistication, and that it will change everything and make existing ways of working obsolete.

Occasionally this is the case. When the motor car was invented, it did succeed in fundamentally changing the world. The car caught on, and horses trotted off. But substitutions such as this are rare, more typically what happens is that the new invention arrives, is found to be good but different to what is already around (rather than a replacement). And so the newcomer snuggles up alongside the existing technologies and you get another book on the shelf, rather than fewer books.

When TV arrived, the death of reading and the radio was foretold, but neither came to pass. The fact is that while television is very popular indeed, you can't watch it while you are driving, doing the ironing or taking a shower, in the way that you can listen to the radio, for example. Similarly, the power of TV has failed to replace the journey of imagination that only reading a novel or poetry can provide.

Of course, while technologies change, we do not. We discover that we still like our old formats, because they still suit us. We hold on to types of communication even if they are old fashioned because they still provide us with benefits that the new formats do not totally deliver.

The same could be said of the Internet. It has brought us some beneficial new features, but it too has its limitations. It is slow, you need to have relatively expensive, dedicated equipment, it is indiscriminate in the sheer size and scale of information available, the technology is extremely unreliable compared to other gadgets in our home, it is difficult to use compared to our radios and TVs, the quality of much of the material is poor, it is still not particularly portable and there are very few trusted and respected brands that we can turn to in the way we can in the real world.

However, it does have some good points, such as speed and ease of gaining information if you can find the location of what you are looking for, the ability to search globally for goods, the opportunity to interact with other people and organizations in a new, low cost, speedy manner, and – for businesses – there is the prospect of increasing sales and reducing costs by reaching bigger audiences, building loyalty and sales as well as removing complexity and cost from the supply chain.

While the Internet is new and presents us with many things to think about, it is not surprising that its effects may not be as cataclysmic as was once thought to be the case. Talk of the Internet changing the world, and being as significant a development as the discovery of printing, now seems rather excitable, given the dot.com crashes that we have seen. However, the Internet is here to stay, it has made a difference and, as the technology improves and simplifies, you do not need to be clairvoyant to see that it will have an increasing impact.

The Internet has only just started to make its presence felt and, in many ways, the fact that the first bubble has burst is probably beneficial. Expectations have now been recalibrated, so that as new wireless and interactive technology comes online, we will now be more realistic about the speed and capabilities of these new developments.

My view is that this will lead to a greater enthusiasm for these technologies as opposed to the apathy that greeted developments such as WAP, which was a huge letdown when it finally arrived. If you overhype anything, the short-term publicity rush leads to major withdrawal symptoms when the product finally arrives and the delight is not delivered as promised. There is a risk that consumers will be far less enthusiastic in the future when they have been disappointed in the past. However, now everyone has woken up from the Internet dream, consumers will hopefully have a clearer head when taking on new technology.

Given that this new technology is with us and will certainly continue to improve and make an increasingly noticeable impact, what does that mean for those who are looking to make the most of this in order to build a winning reputation? What should we be doing about this area, in terms of protecting and promoting the reputation and appeal of our corporation, our brands and ourselves?

The key to understanding how to use new technology in reputation management is partly to understand what that new technology has changed, but also what it has not changed. The Internet has often been talked about as if it was a development on a par with the discovery of electricity, penicillin or the motor car. Internet zealots have not only been able to talk people into investing millions in their dreams, but have also worked their way into our imaginations. However, when it comes to managing reputation, there are a few home truths that need to be spelt out.

First, the same guidelines about managing reputation and public relations apply on the Internet as much as they do in every other walk of PR life. You are still looking to build trust and acceptance in this new electronic world and that requires the same golden rules of good reputation behaviour.

If you want to attain a good reputation, you need to be a respected, interesting organization that engages in a credible and engaging way with your audiences. You need to understand what your audiences are looking for and tune into their needs in terms of providing a communications service. You need to act with integrity and do all the things to manage your reputation online as you would do off-line.

Internet-nots

Clearly there are differences to online reputation management, which we shall come on to, but in fact there are far more similarities. There are also a lot of myths and fairy tales about the Internet that need to be understood in order for reputation warriors to know how to fight effectively in this new theatre of PR war.

First, there is a view that the Internet is alive 24 hours a day, 7 days a week. Like a terrible mechanical monster, it never sleeps and needs constant feeding and watering, otherwise it will create havoc when you are tucked up in bed or on a weekend vacation trip. The truth is that it is no more 24/7 than anything else in life. People still, despite the Internet, need to sleep, have holidays and weekends and the Internet has not changed this. You still need to provide 24-hour, 7-day-a-week PR cover, but this was necessary before the Internet. I am not aware that, because of the Internet, there has been any real increase in the hours worked by PR people. The vision of PR teams working 24-hour shifts like car factory workers simply has not occurred. The reputation world still works on time zones, with the exception of occasional major global announcements, but these mean you will be up all night, Internet or not.

The second misunderstanding about the Internet is that it instantly turns you into a global business, opening you up to world-wide customer and communications audiences. Yes, in theory the whole world can now see and visit your website, but just because they can, does not mean that they do.

It is estimated that there are almost three billion websites on the Internet world-wide. It is a sobering thought to think of how much commotion there is out there, when you are launching a website. Just because you are on the World Wide Web, does not make you world class. First, if your site is in English, you are only global to those countries and people that speak English. Second, if nobody knows you are on the Web, then you are not really global, in fact you are not really anywhere.

While you may have a clever electronic brochure that connects to your e-commerce site, despatch warehouse and so on, your target audience still needs to know that your site exists and why they should visit it. Being there is not enough, you need to be seen to be there and let people know how to find you. The truth is that the fundamental techniques needed to make PR work with the Internet are quite traditional.

If you want your audiences to go to your site, you need to let them know it is there in just the same way that you would need to let people know about your new restaurant that you want them to visit or a new drink that you want them to consume. The rules are the same and you will need to use traditional off-line communications to promote your electronic communications channel.

However, while succeeding in driving your target audiences to your website requires traditional methods of communications, how you handle them once they are there does require the application of a few new ground rules and common-sense laws. First of all, it is important to remember what the experience of using a website is like compared to other types of communications and adapt your style accordingly.

You should bear in mind that looking at a site is essentially a solitary process, it can induce a feeling of loneliness and isolation from society. Unlike other forms of media, such as TV, newspapers, films, magazines and so on, which create a community feel, the Internet is a solo pursuit. Even given all the talk of virtual communities, communication on the Internet is largely a one-to-one relationship.

This has advantages, for example it means that you can develop highly personalized communications, tailor your information and build up an intimate knowledge of your consumers. Throughout, the fact that it is a one-on-one communications channel should influence the style of communications used. The Internet is a personal message delivery system, so it should look and feel like a conversation between two people, not like a mass communication broadcast.

Second, you need to remember that using the Internet can be slow, frustrating, time consuming and complicated. There are barriers to Internet website entry, for example to find the right site you will probably use a search engine (around 80% of people find sites through a search engine), you need to have a browser that is compatible with the search engine, you will need to get onto the site, you may have to register, and then you will have to search around the site for information.

If you have any questions, you can only send an email – how long will it be before it is answered? Will the reply answer all the queries or will it throw up more? Basically, there are many occasions when it is going to be easier to pick up the phone and simply speak to someone. Before you convert all your communications to the Web, you should think this through and remember that the Web is not a panacea. People will still need to call you and talk to spokespersons. The Web is a useful tool, but it should never replace existing communications channels that are working well.

Instead, you should consider how people access information now, and consider how the Internet can enhance that process, rather than simply switching everything to the Web as an alternative to what you currently have. Instead of the only place, the Internet is another place to communicate with your target audiences.

Media meltdown

The Internet has driven a significant change in the way that the media operates, which has important implications for PR professionals. The fact is that today there are far more media outlets, but the same number of journalists serving a larger number of online and off-line publications. This means that the same journalists will be writing for several publications, so cross-pollination of stories across different type of media is likely. That is why we are seeing more stories run from a trade publication story to a national online story, into a radio piece, onto a TV slot and then into a daily print newspaper and finally a weekly magazine.

A relatively small number of journalists covering an ever-expanding media also means there is less time to put stories together, so easily accessible information that is available instantaneously is going to be preferable as source material.

The other factor is that the online media has made speed a new dimension in the media relations universe. Online publications do not have a deadline, they are always on a deadline as any time is publication time. This means that when you deal with online media, you need to be ready to act instantly.

Another driver of change is that while there are the same number of journalists working for more publications, there are actually fewer stories in the media. Although journalists will proudly talk about the importance of scoops and exclusive stories, this is a myth that does not reflect the reality of how the media operates. Rather than operating exclusively, the media works like a swarm, with all print, broadcast and online media essentially covering the same stories all the time.

Try a simple experiment – go out and buy every national newspaper in your country and go through them. They will all be carrying the same news stories, but told from a social, economic and cultural perspective that is pertinent to their readers. The same applies to the day's TV, radio and online fodder. It will be the same stories, because the media works in a pack. The fact is that the views of a nation are formed by a media that is unified in the stories it chooses to cover.

What is in the media is in the collective consciousness. It can be fascinating to spend two weeks reading a foreign newspaper. You will soon find yourself totally out of touch with the vast majority of the everyday conversations going on around you, as you break contact with the national news agenda. This is an issue for PR people in that if there are fewer stories, there are fewer opportunities to secure coverage for yourself or your business. However, it also means that if you have a hit with one journalist, it is likely to create an epidemic of coverage.

The lesson for those people managing media online is that there are no real barriers between the types of media, and the convergence of journalists' areas of interest means that you need to see all journalists as a homogeneous group, because they increasingly are.

However, it is unwise to put too much emphasis on Internet-based journalists as they still lag behind the traditional media brands in terms of audience appeal. Most people today still receive their information from TV, newspapers, radio and magazines. The Internet is not that popular a source of information compared to more established channels. The real issue is that the nature of the Internet makes it relatively inaccessible, compared to most other media. The best way of communicating to people via the net is to push information out rather than sit and wait for the public to come to visit you. This is an important observation for when you are trying to reach journalists as well as when you are attempting to use the Web to communicate outwards yourself – we shall cover this in more detail later in the chapter.

When dealing with online journalists, the basic rules of engagement are the same as with other journalist groups. They require good quality news material and they are looking for high quality, innovative and relevant photography. Online journalists want access to spokespeople with something to say. They work to a new type of deadline and like spokespeople and companies who understand that pressure. Therefore it is important that you are available for online journalists 24 hours a day; however, this is no different to off-line media contacts.

One factor that is different, is that online journalists have a high expectation about the access they will have to major corporations and the speed in which they expect a response. Therefore, it is essential to have the telephone numbers of key spokespeople on material sent to online journalists and for those spokespeople to be available and ready with their key messages to fire back answers and deliver an engaging interview.

This need for speed is simply the product of the different type of deadlines that online journalists work with, that is, immediate and constant. If you are putting your CEO up as a spokesperson, his or her cell phone number needs to be in the material and that person needs to be ready to take that call and start talking fast and to the point. Online journalists will not want an appointment in the diary for a few days hence, they want to speak to your top man now, or they will go elsewhere. This difference in attitude of online journalists needs to be understood and accommodated by ensuring that your company culture can cope with this new way of responding.

Businesses need to be constantly on the starting blocks ready to spring into PR action mode. An online TV crew can be at your office and, due to digital technology, their interview can be on air in minutes. This is fast and the shock waves will ripple out to other media and other stakeholder groups with alarming speed. The lesson here is that you always need to be in control and one step ahead of the media to ensure that the first place your other stakeholder groups hear about any major news is from you, not from the media.

Your online information service

Every company should have a website, as should every initiative, campaign, governing body or pressure group. Even if you have nothing more than an electronic brochure online, there is an expectation that you should be providing information on your company in an easy to read format.

As a basic minimum, your site should include:

▪ Information about your company

▪ Details of products and services offered, with photographs, prices and product specifications

- Company history, values, philosophy

- Details of key personnel, including biographies and photographs, with email addressees

- Address, phone, fax and email details to allow stakeholders to contact you

- Details of distribution – how consumers can purchase your services or products

- Details of after sales service and any other services provided

- Answers to frequently asked questions

- Archive materials for journalists, for example company press releases, copies of announcements, speeches made, details of company structure

- Background information on your products, for example where and how they are made, key features and differences between your offerings and those of your competitors

- Items of interest, for example your views on issues of the day or your responses to industry debates and relevant news items

- Online order forms to place requests for products and services

- It may be relevant to have online order checking facilities, for example to check the status of your account or location of your order

- Career opportunities for those interested in working for your organization

- Hot links to other relevant sites

- Details of other offices, distributors and outlets internationally

- There may be special password-protected sections of the site for privileged customers

- Details of other services and features, for example delivery times or office hours.

Many sites offer a great deal more than this. Interactive games, video, audio, news, chatrooms and downloadable graphics and software are some of the other frequently encountered elements on sites. As you can see, a typical website goes beyond being a simple reputation development and protection mechanism. A modern site is an order taker, information provider, database, archive, electronic HR department, library and talking point.

However, the website does play a critical part in your overall reputation. Its accessibility and style will say a great deal about your corporate culture and market positioning and it can deliver benefits on many layers:

- *Media:* the latest polls show that around 80% of journalists visit websites as their first source of information on companies.

- *Research:* students, pressure groups, analysts, competitors, government researchers and potential employees are just a few of the groups that visit your websites to gather data. Providing background material over the net will save you time and money.

- *Interaction with consumers/data collection:* the Internet website is a superb way to collect data about your customers and provide them with answers to questions. One recent example of how effective such gathering and use of data can be was an online poll conducted by Music.com, a site specializing in pop music. The site asked its users to enter an online poll to see which Spice Girl would have the first number one single. Within eight hours, they had collected customer data on thousands of individuals who were clearly interested in this area and would be predisposed to future communication on related products. In addition, they were able to email and push information to these people at a later date, helping to increase products and loyalty through regular dialogue. The final benefit came when Music.com used the findings of the survey as the basis for a news release, gaining valuable publicity for the site. All this was completed in hours, a task that in the past could have taken at least a week.

- *Creating news:* You can use the Internet to release statements and speeches which can then be promoted in the traditional off-line media. This is similar to the technique of using a conference speech to generate coverage, that is, using an event as the platform for a news announcement, along the lines of: 'Speaking at a gathering of industry leaders … a major announcement was made'.

- *Delivery of information:* this can save your communications team considerable time and effort by answering basic questions and setting out facts in a clear way that avoids misunderstanding and unnecessary calls to the company.

- *A caring/helpful perception for your brand:* high quality, customer-friendly, online support can significantly improve your reputation as helpful and accessible. Online dialogue can provide useful feedback which can be fed into improvements in products and processes.

Making the trip worthwhile

The fact remains that you will still need to use traditional off-line promotional and PR techniques to take people to the site. Unless you trade in something where people will naturally seek information, for example music, films, books and so on, people will not come looking for your site, but it is not an issue as long as you commit sufficient off-line resources to drive traffic online.

When people do visit your site, they need to have an engaging and fulfilling experience. Then they will feel better about your brand and your company and may even return to the site again. So, if you are a sugar manufacturer and you have recipes on your site but do not promote them, nobody will ever go there and your recipes' ingredients will remain on the shelves. However, if you have an on-pack promotion that requires consumers to visit the site to participate, they will then see the recipes and enjoy them and, while they are at it, they may buy the book that you are selling on the subject, order a set of saucepans, read about the sugar manufacturing process, read about the stock price performance of the company or scan an interview with a celebrity on his favourite sugar-based recipes.

By moving in this direction, you are creeping into new territory where you are becoming a media provider yourself. There is absolutely no reason why companies should not be the source of a high standard of editorial information. This is, after all, simply the online extension of customer newsletters and magazines, many of which are extremely successful and well read. As in the off-line world, the same rules apply – people will respond to well-crafted, visually appealing and truly informative editorial, whoever provides it. Dull, overtly commercial and biased output will be ignored as corporate propaganda and will make no meaningful impact on your target audiences' behaviour and attitudes towards your brand, your company or its offerings.

However, if you can deliver high-quality editorial content that entertains, informs and educates, you will, at the end of it, have a loyal consumer that has undergone a full brand experience. You may also have earned some revenue. But without the quality content, combined with a traditional on-pack offer, our sugar firm's brand values and hi-tech wizardry would have remained in the dark. And remember, in hyperspace no one can hear your dream.

Sales/lead generation

The above example shows how some sales can be generated on the back of what is essentially a reputation building initiative. However, the Internet can be used purely to drive sales figures as well as reputation scores. Traditional off-line techniques, such as editorial coverage, advertisements or direct mail, can be used to push people to your site where they can enter their personal details, for example via a prize draw or an online competition. Email and mobile phone numbers are especially valuable to harvest, as these can be used later on to reach out to these consumers. Tailored emails can be regularly distributed to customers, or you can push out text messages to mobile phones on a mass basis to alert people to special offers and company news.

Internal communications

Your Intranet site (a password-protected site available only to employees) can be a useful way to communicate with employees. Such sites can be helpful as mechanisms to send out news and information, providing a place for employees to share knowledge and best practice, and offering a location for information to be held, along with examples of similar projects, guidelines on handling issues, policies and recommendations. An Intranet site can contain details of company talents and experience. Photographs, technical drawings, artwork and graphics can also be stored online for easy, instant access.

Webcasts, news pages and video and audio streams can be employed to make announcements and break company news. Details of internal schemes such as employee volunteering as well as sports and social events can also be included online.

One word of caution – Intranet communications should not be used as the only means of internal communications. Especially if your company has a culture of face-to-face and cascade briefings, moving totally to an electronic method of internal communications will not be successful. Intranets are best combined with traditional internal communications techniques such as notice boards, local team briefings and face-to-face conversations.

However, there is no doubt that electronic internal communications can be especially helpful when there is a strong email culture or a disparate workforce, perhaps due to a high number of home workers or multinational employees who need to be brought together. In these cases an

Intranet, coupled with traditional internal communications techniques, can be very effective for internal communications and as a platform for improved working procedures.

Opinion former/stakeholder communications

While an Intranet is a password-protected site for employees, Extranet is a password-protected site for people outside your organization. This can be a very useful reputation management tool. For example, you can populate the site with a membership list of opinion formers, political contacts, journalists, key customers, pressure groups, conference organizers, recruitment consultants, analysts and so on – all the key audiences that matter to your business.

Not only can you use this as you would a traditional database, that is, for email shots and sending out regular information, but you can also create a site containing useful data for these important audiences. Research papers, commentary on relevant issues, company information, details of new investments, relevant personnel, company products and history can all be included and made available to these special friends of the business.

You can also use this site to provide hot links to other relevant sites, for example to opinion forming and authoritative sites that you know are supportive of your arguments, your product or service. Remember that you should always ask permission to put in a hyperlink, especially if this is with an organization with which you wish to be seen to be co-operating.

In some countries this is not mandatory under law, for example the US, but in others, such as the UK, it is a legal requirement. Regardless of the law, it is advisable to request permission in order to build up goodwill. Some organizations will agree readily, but some will consent only to provide links that go into their site but not from their site to your own.

Content, content, content

The question is not so much whether you should have a website, but what should be on it. It is difficult to imagine saying that you do not have a site in today's business world, as that admission alone would put a dent in your reputation. However, the real test is how relevant and useful the content of your site is for stakeholders.

The main factors are:

1. *Relevance:* ensure your site is tailored to local markets and issues. For example, do not have an Intranet site that flags up American national holidays only, as you will alienate all your non-US employees. Keep product and other information locally relevant and always ensure that company contact details are local and not simply those in the company's head office country.

2. *Openness:* information should be frank, easy to follow and to find. Details should be forthcoming with plenty of accurate data about the business, covering what it does and where it stands on issues of the day.

3. *Credibility:* as with all communications, the information on your site needs to be credible and believable and backed up with facts and figures throughout, in order to ensure that what you are saying is robust and convincing.

4. *Ease of use:* websites should look good, be easy to navigate, stimulating, eye catching and well constructed. The style of communications on the Web is very important. The language you use needs to be friendly, accessible and conversational. Remember that people using your site will probably be sitting on their own in front of a screen. It is a solitary one-to-one communications experience – a conversation – so try and adopt that tone in your language and style of communications.

Visual connections

The Internet is a visual media and when designing a website you need to think in terms of pictures and sounds as well as text. Moving images can be widely received, as can audio so, for example, you can have spokespeople actually giving radio interviews on audio, which can be taken digitally by radio stations. Graphics can also be used to explain complex structures or processes and can be effective ways to move people around your site, by drawing them into other zones of interest.

Generally, it is best to offer your users the highest possible technical standards as more and more people have broadband Internet connections and most can receive moving images and high quantities of data. This will become the standard in the future, so aim to provide such a level of sophistication today.

Online issues and crisis management

One of the major differences effected by the Internet is an expectation of transparency. External and internal stakeholders assume that they will be able to find all the global information about your organization on the Web.

This presents two challenges. First, you need to live up to this reputation expectation and ensure that you provide details of your chief executive and other senior people, their contact details, pictures, biographies and so on. But you also need to cover information around more sensitive issues such as prices around the world, ingredients used, environmental policies and performance, your activities in the local community, details of consumer sales offers and employment conditions.

This introduces the issue of dealing with any inconsistencies that this transparency reveals. For example, your prices around the world will undoubtedly vary. If you visit the Nikon camera website, you can choose which country website you visit and you will see the same camera available at different prices in different markets. With world-wide guarantees, back-up service, payment and delivery services, it is hard to comprehend why anyone should simply not buy from the cheapest market.

Clearly, companies need to be able to handle the questions and the consequences of these apparent contradictions. A great deal can be explained by local taxes and other conditions, but sometimes companies are left with limited arguments in defence of their pricing and other policies. This can be made much tougher when your opponent is also your distributor. For example, Levi Strauss, the jeans manufacturer, is locked in a dispute with Tesco, a major UK retailer. The row, which is being played out and amplified online as well as in off-line media, political and legal circles, centres on Tesco's desire to sell Levi's at a lower price in the UK than Levi would like. Levi's concern is the effect that bargain basement prices will have on the perception of its brand as well as the adverse effect that Tesco's policy will have on the other UK retailers who are not in a position to put loss-leading campaigns into place.

The Internet is both a useful and dangerous place where these debates can be managed. The real point of looking at the Internet as a forum is that the Internet can often spill into the mainstream media or be used as evidence by decision makers, for example lawyers or political leaders. The Internet in itself is not important, but it is a vital feeder source into other more influential media and decision-making processes.

Avoiding trouble by ensuring as far as possible that your own site does not contain the inconsistencies and pitfalls that could get your company into deep water, is the first step to issues management and crisis avoidance on the Web. Given that your own site is under your control, this should be an achievable goal. The site needs to be subject to the same reputational scrutiny as the rest of your communications to ensure that there are no weak spots and your points of view are as robustly defended as possible.

The next step in online reputation management is to look at sites other than your own to see how relevant issues and your own reputation is being handled. The first place to look is your own distributors' sites. This will not be relevant for all companies, but many organizations rely on a network of partly owned or totally independent businesses to distribute and sell their products and services. Dealers, wholesalers, distributors, retailers, agents, franchises and individuals will be out there using your identity, your products and your brand in their own communications.

You need to be sure that they are representing you in ways that you approve of: visually, in terms of logos and use of corporate identity; factually, regarding prices, ingredients lists, accuracy of service and product details; and stylistically, is the tone correct for your brand and what you stand for? Providing this distribution network with high-quality, central guidelines on content and visual identity will be welcomed in most cases. Time needs to be spent working with your partners to ensure that they show off your company to its best advantage. However, if such positive support fails to make a difference, then legal action is often needed to protect your interests and your reputation.

The next ripple in the Internet pond is sites that are run by organizations and individuals totally beyond your control. Opposition groups, trade bodies, competitors, media sites, anti-sites, sites run by individuals, governments and other influential organizations are all examples of the sources of information on the Web that could be talking about you and your products. What are they saying? How much of it is lies? Who is sticking up for you? And who is sticking the knife in you?

The fact is, you need to know what they are saying about you down at the Internet gossip shops. Finding out the word on the Web is actually relatively simple and increasingly inexpensive or free. As well as the established Internet monitoring companies that charge for their service, there are a growing number of online companies where you can type in details of your company or area of interest and they will – at no charge – tell you in which chat groups and sites you are being discussed right now.

The problem is not so much knowing who is talking, but knowing what to do about it. Given that there are so many chat groups and newsgroups that nobody has been able to count them (it is estimated that tens of millions exist and they are always increasing, never disappearing), it is likely that there is a lot of chatter, but how much of it matters? And what should you act on and what should you ignore?

The answer is that the same rules of reputation and issues management apply in Cyberia as they do in Siberia. If you are being attacked in chat rooms and on anti-sites, you need to compile the same analysis as you would do elsewhere. Who is behind the site? What is their agenda? You need to segment the critical and the supportive audiences, understand their motivations and then look to see if there is any common ground from which you can build greater understanding and co-operation.

Generally, it is best not to have this dialogue online. Face-to-face meetings should be sought to discuss issues raised rather than seeking to battle it out in public on the Web, where there is a strong likelihood that you will simply come across as defensive and complaining. Face-to-face communications, if possible, are always a far superior way to communicate and build understanding.

Anti-sites and negativity in chat rooms and newsgroups need careful handling, and tactics vary. Some companies attempt to answer their critics directly, but this is rarely advisable – face-to-face diffusion of opposition is always preferable. However, some have opened their arms to their anti-sites and recognized that they can be useful ways to gain consumer feedback and hear about issues that are genuine problems that need to be put right.

IKEA, the Swedish furniture retailer, and Dunkin Donuts, the global restaurant chain, have both taken welcoming stances to their anti-sites, frequently thanking contributors for comments and implementing many suggestions. Both sites have taken the decision to collect customer information and feedback which is then fed into the business decision-making processes and into training and product development.

Shell has taken a different approach to embracing its critics by having hot links from its own site to those that hold alternative views, as well as developing a full section on the site that answers critical emails and addresses negative issues in a way that allows the business to put its point of view across.

Some companies ignore their anti-sites. This can be the correct policy if the site is clearly so hardline that it cannot be influenced or if the site is actually not that harmful and to be seen to be crushing it would backfire. The most celebrated example of corporate overreaction was McDonald's off-line PR error of suing two obscure, fringe extremists who were handing protest leaflets out in North London streets, accusing the company of a range of environmental, social and cultural transgressions.

The result was the longest libel case in British legal history, a lawyers' bill for millions of dollars, bundles of negative media coverage and the setting up of one of the world's most established anti-sites. The company had turned a small North London dispute into a global reputation catastrophe and elevated two marginal activists into anti-capitalist icons. McDonald's won the case overall, but the cost was high in terms of corporate distraction, financial expense and reputation stress.

McDonald's overreacted on that occasion, but when significant, critical sites or newsrooms are spreading serious misinformation, a company has no option other than to defend its position and try and respond to its critics. This is a task that may take many years and will perhaps never be completed in many cases. But, reputation abhors a vacuum and if you do not speak up for yourself, people will assume the worst. The challenge is to defend, but also to avoid escalation and confrontation. As Winston Churchill said, 'jaw jaw is better than war war' and the same applies to the net and all aspects of reputation management.

As in all other areas of reputation management, the fact is that you have very little choice other than to respond to criticism and misinformation. You should always remember that your reputation headstone is constantly being recarved. Whatever the last thing people said about you in the media is how you will be remembered. And yesterday's news never goes away, thanks to the Internet – ever. Your past reputation contained in media coverage from history is the starting point for everyone who comes to talk to you or who is considering working for you, or buying into your brand or corporate standpoint.

And it is not just journalists that can access old media cuttings to prepare for meetings. The Internet means that everyone can get a potted history of you and your business. Now every potential customer, hopeful recruit, analyst, opponent, competitor and government official, can go to, for example, Reuters or to FT.com and get cuttings going back years, not just from major national newspapers, but from trade publications and specialist journals around the world. It is an unnerving experience to see a graduate or a journalist arrive for an interview clutching a pile of cuttings about you going back throughout your career. If it has not happened to you yet, it will. And when it does, you better be ready with an answer for anything written on you or your business in the past and anywhere in the world.

It is your job to be constantly refreshing that history of yourself and your business, as held in cuttings archives. If you have had a negative media period in your personal or corporate life, you need to put clear blue water between then and now, by topping up the cuttings files with some good news. It takes time and effort to leave a negative perception in the dust, but the more good news there is between you and the bad times in the rear view mirror, the better.

On a more positive note, third-party support can often be built effectively on the net, for example the scientific community is highly Internet literate and online discussions with opinion former groups such as this can be cultivated to counterbalance the views of your most extreme critics.

The process of tagging issues as red, amber and green as discussed in Chapter 4 applies equally to the Internet, where you will need to establish a new process to manage the immense quantity of material that is likely to be circulating about you, your brands and your business. Only then will you have a rational basis to guide your reactions to reputation challenges on the net, allowing you to decide what needs an answer and what needs nothing other than a watchful eye.

You need to be vigilant and ensure that you spot those occasions when a green tagged issue starts to turn amber and begins to develop red tinges. Sometimes the most obscure issues can ferment into big news. Occasionally issues germinate in other countries or within small specialist communities. Then a mainstream journalist or campaigner picks it up and places it centre stage in the public – normally off-line – conscience. One example was five years ago when Intel, the chip manufacturer, suffered a collapse of its share price following the explosion of a low profile issue, concerning problems being faced by a number of IT professionals. The company knew about it, but failed to act in a sufficiently robust way. Everything was quiet until a trade journalist picked up the story and it transferred to the national media, with serious financial and reputational consequences. Remember, it may look like a little issue now, but if neglected it can mutate into something very ugly indeed.

Chat room etiquette

Should you decide to cut into chat rooms to make a point, there are a few rules that need to be observed. First, you should probably not barge into chat rooms and start stomping your corporate feet around the place. It will most likely escalate the situation and make other participants see red. Face-to-face contact with the ringleaders is always preferable. Alternatively, managing issues in the off-line media, in order to shape the online debate, is another preferable route.

The second key point is that, in the same way that only authorized spokespeople from your company speak to the traditional media or opinion former networks, the same rule must apply online. It should be clearly communicated to all employees that it is a sackable offence to participate in chat rooms or elsewhere online as a company representative.

The third rule is that you should never enter a chat room and claim to be anything other than a company representative. If you pretend to be a civilian, you will get found out and the corporate embarrassment will be immense.

The dark side of the boom

Whether to manage issues that 'go large' or to handle serious crises, it is worth setting up dark sites as part of your reputation protection arsenal. These sites are the reputational equivalent of nuclear war bunkers – empty places on the net that are fully equipped and waiting to be used if a full-scale crisis occurs.

Dark sites provide a ready-made, single point of information and contact for crises that is away from your main site, which can be up and running within hours of a crisis happening. They can be loaded in advance with company information, contacts, biographies, key facts, positioning statements, company data, product recall procedures and media handling services.

An important part of dark sites is that they sit separately from your main sites, so the surge of requests that could result from a crisis are handled elsewhere and do not jeopardize the performance of your existing sites and systems. Dark sites are a modern component in today's crisis preparedness plans, along with crisis manuals and incident rooms, that every PR professional should ensure is available to the business.

The new frontier with the old rules – getting started

Setting up a site is not especially expensive, you can get online from around $5,000 and a very acceptable site can be yours for $15–20,000. There are many design companies that can help you to create your site, but once it is up and running, maintaining it can be done relatively easily in-house.

Once you are online, you have a whole new way to communicate, from webcasts (easily organized with the help of a Web design or PR company) to online chat room participation. You will need to be fast and ever ready, but these are requirements of any person looking to build a strong and vivid reputation for themselves or their business. The online rules are the same as the off-line ones, you can have a winning reputation online if you choose to and the actions you need to take are very similar to those required off-line.

Above all, you need to ensure your off- and online communications are joined up and that you apply the same rigorous standards to your electronic communications as in all other areas. The Internet is not a virtual surrogate for all your real life communication. It plays an important role in reputation management terms, by supporting and stimulating more intimate and traditional communications techniques such as established media relations and face-to-face meetings.

The Internet needs time, attention and almost definitely some external professional expertise to help you to establish yourself in this new zone. There is no doubt that new technology ahead will make the Internet even more interesting to reputation managers and I would encourage those of you who welcome the new spirit of open communications and reputation promotion to see the Internet as a real bonus for creating winning reputations.

It is the duty of communications professionals and everyone concerned with reputational integrity to use the net to set stories straight, to counter misinformation and ignorance. It is imperative that the net delivers its potential as a genuinely useful source for information and dialogue rather than descending into the hands of extremists, junk emailers and proponents of corporate blandness. A strong, credible Internet will help us all to do our job as communicators more effectively. Overall, it is a boon to those who are open and see improved communications as a way to improve the quality of life as well as personal and corporate fortunes. Long live the net!

CHAPTER 9

Spreading your gospel: how to turn your employees into your biggest fans

In the recent reputation management boom, one group of stakeholders has been largely overlooked and that is employees. Although resources allocated to external communications have been growing in size and sophistication, internal communications have been the Cinderella of reputation management.

There have been two reasons for this. First, internal communications is often not driven by the external affairs department in many organizations. Instead, it is frequently managed by the human resources team, where the priority and focus on communications may be different compared to external communications. Second, employees are often seen as second-class citizens when it comes to communication. External audiences are given more resources and priority. Frequently this is due to budget limitations, or a cultural view that employees are an 'easier', captive audience and therefore there is less need to manage communications to this group in as formal a way as to external audiences.

These attitudes are altering gradually as companies realize that change management programmes require a greater commitment to internal communication. Also, organizations are increasingly aware that whatever the brand or service promises being made in their advertising, PR and other communications, the definitive brand experience is often shaped by the consumer's interaction with a member of staff. Regardless of the business processes that you have in place, the final link is often an employee and if that individual does not handle that concluding brand transaction in a way that delights the consumer, then all the upfront investment in product, processes and promotion is undermined. Case Study 10.17 of Railtrack in the UK, is an excellent example of a company that has committed seriously to the process of using internal communications as a key part of delivering its brand and service promise to customers.

So although more emphasis is being placed on managing internal communications as professionally as external interactions, it is still a neglected and underused muscle in most corporate bodies. This is a source for concern for those of us who want to build a winning reputation. As we have seen, one of the most frequently made reputation management errors is to omit an audience group from your communications plans. The minute you have a stakeholder group that is not joined up to your overall reputation management machine, you have the potential for trouble. The marginalized audience group will feel left out and neglected. This can lead to resentment and destructive behaviour as the 'snubbed' group retaliate. Even if they do not actively cause trouble, at best they will be demotivated.

A stakeholder group that is demotivated and reputationally inert is a wasted opportunity. Instead of being resentful drones, your employees could be advocates for the business, disciples spreading the good news gospel and defending the organization in everyday life. In addition, they could be a group of highly motivated individuals that feel positive about who they work for and determined to deliver the best possible service.

Winning this level of support from your employees should be the goal of anyone looking to build a winning reputation. This is particularly important when you consider that a view of an organization, in other words its reputation, is formed as a result of three aspects, namely, what the organization:

1. *looks like:* its image as conveyed in advertising, packaging, vehicles, products, buildings, websites and literature

2. *says:* what the business talks about in the media and the claims it makes in other marketing activity

3. *does:* how it behaves and how it delivers on the promises made.

How the organization acts is critical in ensuring that the business and its brands have a positive relationship with stakeholders. While employee behaviour and attitudes can shape how the company looks and speaks, their role is fairly limited. However, when you look at the 'does' part of your company's reputation, success here is largely out of the hands of the advertising and PR people and firmly with the workers and their ability to deliver your brand promise, day in, day out.

Three steps to turning your employees into evangelists

The primary aim is not to turn employees into advocates for the company, that is the outcome. The way to achieve this is to create a workforce that enjoys its job. A happy workforce will be motivated and this will also lead to more effective, positive communications between employees and external audiences.

As with all aspects of reputation management, the job is to build a better company and then enjoy the improved reputation that follows, rather than try and work at a superficial level, and aim to spin a positive perception, rather than improve reality. The same principle applies to employee communications, only more so, because your employees are the hardest audience to move if you only use slick PR rather than real communications-led changes. Employees are closer to the real world of your organization than any of your other stakeholders. They know you very well and can detect insincerity before anyone else.

On the other hand, your employees are probably the most receptive stakeholder group. For a start, they are interested in the company and in receiving information about it. Typically, they are also responsive to invitations to become more involved in addressing issues. Most people actually want to enjoy their work and make a difference. It is more desirable to work for a successful organization and the majority of employees are willing to respond to company communications and do the best they can.

So employees can be your greatest allies, but they can also be your sternest critics. The task for any leader is to understand the most effective way to activate this reputation fighting force and how to avoid the communications errors that can short-circuit the best-laid internal communications plans.

The challenge involves moving your employees along a three-step path:

- *Step 1: Understanding*
  Employees need to grasp how their job and their activities fit into the bigger picture. Employees must be able to see how their actions and attitudes link to the business's performance. This can be brought to life by feeding back the results of consumer research into satisfaction levels versus competitors as well as factors that influence purchase.

- *Step 2: Acceptance*
  This occurs when your employees have acknowledged that they can shape the company's fortunes by their own actions. Employees will also

need to be inspired at this stage to change and put in place improvements in their performance. In addition, you will need to have introduced new processes to allow change to take place as well as revised ways to evaluate improvement and recognize and reward new behaviours.

■ *Step 3: Support*

This is the Grail that you should be striving for, where your employees are actively supporting the business in their everyday communications, for example with customers, but also with suppliers, competitors, friends and families. Not only are they spreading the communications messages, they will be committed to working in a way that supports the business goals and delivers the highest possible levels of performance against specific objectives.

The symbiotic relationship between PR and HR

It is important to stress that no matter how excellent your internal communications, you will not change employee behaviour through communications alone. You certainly can change attitudes with communications, but behaviour takes more than talk. As in all areas of reputation management, not only do you need to listen and talk more effectively, you also need to change how you do business.

This is as true with internal communications as with all other aspects of reputation management. You cannot move your employees to the support stage using PR alone. You will need help from your HR team. You can lead the horse to water, but you need your human resources team to make it worthwhile for the horse to drink.

The reason why communications alone cannot be relied on to change behaviour is due to human nature. Years of psychologists' studies have given us a reputation management lesson, which is common sense once you think about it. The fact is that just because we know about something does not mean we will do anything about it. Sometimes we will act on new information that we receive from PR, advertising or from third-party endorsement. However, if the change in behaviour requires a short-term sacrifice for a result that may or may not be forthcoming sometime in the future, the likelihood of changing is low.

For example, we all know that it is unhealthy to smoke, drink and not get any exercise. However, many of us still continue to smoke, drink and not go to the gym. Even if we modify our behaviour and reduce the amount that we partake in these vices, we still indulge to an extent in behaviour that we know is bad for us. This is because it is easier not to make the short-term sacrifice, added to which, the benefits of abstaining are uncertain ('I might not get cancer/heart disease') and the consequences, if they occur, are at some indeterminate time in the future. Overall, the motivation to change is relatively low and greatly linked to the personal willpower of each individual.

If one applies this learning to the workplace, you will see how communications alone will also fail to change behaviour. It can make a big difference, but in order to tip employees over the edge into action, you need to offer up a package, and communications is just part of the bundle of measures needed.

This is where your HR team need to work with you to develop a set of reward and recognition structures that motivate appropriate behaviour and curb deviations. These may well be implemented by you as a leader within the business and again it is helpful to understand human nature when putting these internal communications and motivational tools into practice, not least because the rules on how they are best applied can at first appear counterintuitive.

For example, to stop inappropriate employee behaviour, any reprimand or punishment must be both immediate and applied every time the behaviour occurs, without exception. You can see why this works if you think of the analogy of fines for parking violations. If you always get a ticket for parking illegally in a certain street, you will stop trying to park there. If you occasionally receive a ticket, but often get away with it, you are likely to keep on parking there illegally, as there is always a chance you will not be caught.

Conversely, appropriate employee behaviour should be rewarded occasionally and apparently at random. This paradox can be explained through the comparison with gambling. Gambling is appealing to many people because the reward of winning is occasional and unpredictable. If you always get what you want, you stop wanting it as much.

In internal communications terms, this is why apparently random, spontaneous activities such as a handwritten note thanking an employee for excellent work, or the sudden delivery of a case of champagne to every employee's home, will have a far greater impact than regularized reward and recognition schemes such as 'employee of the month', or a regular article in the staff magazine.

By understanding these basics of human motivation, we can work with our HR colleagues to develop internal communications that really deliver results, rather than a process which simply talks to a polite, but closed audience.

Creating an employee communications campaign

Planning

By now you will have grasped that an internal communications programme requires the same level of planning and professionalism as an external campaign. Therefore, as with an external communications programme, you need to begin with the business goals when concocting a programme for staff.

For example, if the business goal is to increase consumer spend per head, then it will be clear what the employee role is in that, perhaps through improved after sales service, better cross-selling of related products and so on. If the business task is to reduce manufacturing costs or improve the rate of innovation, again roles and objectives for employees can be developed to support each objective.

The task of any internal communications programme is to align employee priorities and behaviour with the priorities of customers and the corporation. If employees understand what customers and the business want, they can be mobilized in a way that will make maximum impact to customer satisfaction and the delivery of business goals. All too often, internal communications focus simply on making staff feel happy or well informed. These are unlikely to be business objectives, although they will be part of a strategy to achieve the objectives. It is important to understand the difference, so you, as a reputation creator, can focus on the outcomes of your communications in terms of business results.

With the objectives clear, it will be easier to determine how each objective can be measured. It is essential to work out at the beginning of any campaign how the internal communications activity will be evaluated. It may involve looking at measures such as consumer satisfaction levels, repeat business, staff retention, cost reduction, industry awards won, or fewer consumer complaints. Whatever the measure, agreeing it at the beginning of the programme is critical if you want to evaluate your progress.

Tools for the job

Of all the modes of reputation management, employee communication is perhaps the most dependent on human contact. Employees are not strangers. Even if you have never met them, your staff see you as someone they know. Also, they will certainly know and look to their immediate line manager as the person they rely on to provide them with news and information about the business.

Because of this, your employee communications tactics should involve as much face-to-face contact as possible. In an ideal world, you would be able to sit every employee down for a personal briefing with the CEO. The next best thing is to put everyone in the same room with the CEO. These should be your preferred methods of communications whenever possible. On most occasions, this will not be practical. So the optimal solution is to have face-to-face briefings – individual or all together – with relevant, local line managers, supplemented, on occasion, by a communication from the CEO, via email or video for example.

Line managers themselves need to be motivated and provided with presentation tools, for example a set of PowerPoint slides and speaker notes, to ensure that there is consistency of message, but most importantly to foster infectious enthusiasm among the local managers who will be in the front line.

Other tools such as employee videos, newsletters, emails, and Intranet sites do have a role to play, but it should almost always be a supporting one to supplement face-to-face, local cascade briefing. For example, employee communication materials can be helpful reinforcements to the spoken word: new structures can be explained effectively through clear graphics; video allows everyone to see aspects of the company that could otherwise be difficult to view, such as facilities around the world, or images of customers using products.

Printed or video materials can also be taken home by employees for further scrutiny or to share with friends and family. This also applies to online communications for those with a PC at home. This can help people to absorb the information and can provide handy ammunition in the form of facts and figures to use with people outside the business. Producing a simple fact booklet can help employees to answer frequently asked questions in social or work settings.

Many companies now produce pocket guides for employees to help them to answer questions from friends, family, customers or opponents of the company. Nobody likes to hear their company criticized and the vast majority of employees appreciate being given the wherewithal to answer critics and genuine enquiries with robust, credible answers.

Workers of the world unite ... into market segments

An important factor when thinking about the most effective tone and methods for internal communications is to consider the lifestyles and characteristics of your target audience, in the same way that you would address an external communications challenge.

Many companies have a diverse workforce, that could include unskilled manual workers, highly educated specialists, scientists, lawyers, marketing people, caterers, lorry drivers, shift workers, home workers, non-English speakers, factory workers and a highly driven sales force. As well as this, your company will have a distinct corporate style, such as traditional, high-tech, technophobic, flat, hierarchical, chaotic, structured, centralized and decentralized.

These factors will shape and determine the tools for internal communication that you use, for example email will be pretty ineffective for employees without PCs, but an engineering or technical culture may find Intranets useful. Choosing the method to fit the needs of recipients is not too difficult a task. Some simple pilot research into how people receive information and what their working day is actually like will help to inform your decisions on which tools to choose.

However, while tools will vary, one thing that all employees respond favourably towards is well-written, clear, credible communications. Regardless of level of education or work/lifestyle, employees unite in their rejection of corporate flannel. What is more, you actually want your employees to understand the points you are trying to make, so – as in the external communications arena – keep you key messages punchy, easy to understand and remember.

And above all, ensure that the information that you provide is relevant to the world inhabited by your staff. It is preferable to talk about progress made in areas such as customer satisfaction or new product development rather than focusing on alienating topics such as shareholder value or profits. These are important aspects that you as a leader need to worry about, but your employees are going to be motivated by more immediate factors pertinent to their working day. You take care of Wall Street and let the employees focus on the high street.

Blurred visions and missions

It is important to establish what it is you are expecting from your employees right from the start. Ongoing cascade briefings, newsletters and so on will be far more effective if they are set against a context of what the business is trying to achieve overall.

Clear visions also provide motivation and inspiration for people as well as a road map for the future. A sense of direction is something we all need and it is your job as a reputation maker to provide that ambition for your staff.

Although there can be variations to this, I would recommend that the key elements of any foundation staff communication should include:

- *Vision:* this is a picture of how you see the future in relation to your customers, if you are successful as an organization. As always, try and keep the wording short, motivational and relevant to your target audience (not related to what you do, but more towards what you provide). So if you were an advertising agency, your vision might be 'that every one of our clients' products is a favourite household name'

- *Mission:* this is more related to what you do as a business, for example, sticking with the advertising agency example, the mission could be 'to create work that makes our clients smile and consumers buy'

- *Goals:* these relate to how you will get there, 'to employ the best creative minds in advertising', for example. Aim to have no more than three goals, as it is difficult to focus on more

- *Objectives:* this provides more specific supporting information. At our advertising agency it could be 'to provide an atmosphere where creative excellence is rewarded and encouraged'

- *Strategy:* this is about how you will get there. Sticking with the advertising agency example, the strategy could be 'by establishing a creative training programme that guarantees 400 hours a year of training per person'

- *Actions:* self-explanatory, but this section sets out in detail what everyone must do to deliver the strategy, personally, as teams and as a company

- *Measures:* clear indications of how progress will be measured. In the case of improved creativity in our advertising agency example, the measures could be 'to win at least four creativity awards and see our creativity rating increase by 10% in the annual client satisfaction survey'.

A great deal of time will be spent consulting with colleagues and co-workers on arriving at these key statements, but it will be time well spent, because a group of people that is clear about what it is trying to achieve and how it will get there is a powerful collective, even more so, if that plan has been arrived at in a way in which participants feel that they have been consulted and have had the opportunity to shape their own work plan for the future. As a reputation leader, it is your role, along with your HR colleagues and others in your reputation consultative group, to take the workforce through this process of self-determining their future trajectory as a team.

Putting on a show for the troops

With all your plans and processes in place, it is important to remember the other rule about communications, which is that creativity and colour are critical to catch people's attention and engage their hearts and minds. What is sauce for the external goose is just as needed for the internal gander and it is important not to fall at the last fence by neglecting to make your internal communications as motivational and appealing as you would for outsiders.

But before we look at how you communicate, I want to touch briefly on when. The rules here are simple. First, you should have your internal communications machine set up now, as you do not want to be establishing processes in times of stress, such as a merger or a crisis. Employees need to trust and be familiar with the process, so establish your channels and formats now, do not wait until 'you have something to announce'.

Second, your communications should be regular and repetitive. As with all audiences, saying the same thing every month rather than something different every month is far more effective. You will be sick of making the same speech every time, but your audience will need to hear you say the same thing many times, before it seeps into their consciousness. You also need to remember that holidays and conflicting priorities mean that not everyone will see every one of your communications, so the greater the frequency of repetition, the greater the chance of messages hitting home.

Once the processes are established, you can think about style. Two-way dialogue is important in all communications, but especially with employees. Suggestion schemes, focus groups, working parties, off-site away days and consultation will give employees a sense that they are making their voice heard and shaping the thinking within the organization. You need to be ready to respond to suggestions and be seen to be considering them seriously, even if they are not fully implemented. In this area of reputation management, it is the thought that counts.

Another useful device is to focus initiatives around campaigns. These can be branded and should always be fairly short lived, with a clear goal in mind, for example 'cut accidents by 10% this month'. An important consideration is not to have too many initiatives of this nature, as campaign inflation will occur and effort becomes dissipated by 'the flavour of the month' factor. However, when used sparingly, campaigns can provide very effective hubs around which effort can be structured.

In execution, remember that employees respond as consumers do to striking visuals, creative slogans and engaging copy. Don't skimp on using creative talent when putting together campaigns, just because it is a performance for your own staff. Similarly, remember the effect that a touch of glamour and humour can have on us all, for example the involvement of celebrities or humorous cartoons can galvanize a workforce communications initiative.

Keep in mind the power of the media, and aim to co-ordinate internal announcements with external media coverage. Your employees are more likely to believe what they read about your organization in the external media than in the company publications. You should ensure, therefore, that there is as much consistency and reinforcement as possible across all types of media and internal communications, by co-ordinating messages and timing as far as is practicable.

Finally, remember that, as a leader within the business, you can help to drive reputational perceptions by having a high profile yourself. Employees enjoy seeing their boss in the media or speaking at events. Employees want to think that they work for a leading thinker in their field or a high profile micro celebrity. This will engender pride in your staff and strengthen your call to action.

Having a high visibility in the business helps to motivate employees, and external media exposure will amplify any personal visits and create a feeling that every employee knows you personally. Having a profile that is both high and appealing will go a long way to motivating the people who work for you. They will, as a result, be more amenable to adopt a style of working that helps the business to achieve its overall goals. This in turn will lead to a reputation improvement.

And there is another personal dividend that employee motivation will pay out, which is that your own personal reputation will be enhanced, as a result of having a workforce of supporters, in focus groups and on the shop floor, all singing your praises as a leader.

Third-party endorsement of your business and yourself is one of the key goals for those dedicated to building a winning reputation. The support of employees is a special type of third-party endorsement which is often neglected, but, when it is focused and harnessed, provides you with an army of advocates to take your messages to the furthest outposts of the commercial world.

CHAPTER 10

Winning reputation case studies: learning from the best

Gestetner digital art experience

GESTETNER

Although a major European digital office equipment company, Gestetner was perceived as old fashioned and out of date. Gestetner's leadership in innovative digital technology was not known by IT managers. During 1998–99 Gestetner had a window of opportunity presented by the launch of a new product range, which put them ahead of the competition in the world of digital technology.

The company conducted research which showed that 'digital' was identified as a key word to link with Gestetner in order to win a cutting-edge image. An association with digital art was identified as an interesting way to demonstrate Gestetner's focus on leading-edge technology. The Communication Group (Gestetner's PR consultancy on this project) researched the leading digital art experts and established links with the London-based Royal College of Art (RCA), the London Science Museum and the Institute of Contemporary Arts, all with strong media visibility and an Internet presence.

The objective of the campaign was to position Gestetner at the cutting edge of digital technology and communicate this to key commercial targets, identified as IT managers in the commercial sector, and procurement specialists in major commercial accounts and the public sector. A list of 10,000 contacts was compiled, and the timetable for the initiative established, starting with the launch of the challenge to RCA students, through to adjudication and an exhibition of winners.

The contest was launched at the Science Museum and the winner was announced at the RCA. Julie Freeman, a leading digital artist, won the competition and produced the Gestetner Digital Wave. Her work created an interactive, visually spectacular work of art which could be reproduced on Gestetner colour printers and shirts, as well as in the accompanying press materials.

Broadcast publicity on BBC 1's *Tomorrow's World* and *Blue Peter*, as well as other electronic media, reached an audience of over 10 million. Press coverage reached a circulation of 3 million, and the Gestetner Digital Wave appeared on four Internet websites. The target commercial audience of 10,000 received six mailings in connection with the promotion. During the period of the campaign, sales of Gestetner's products increased by 25% in the UK, the highest growth ever achieved.

CASE STUDY 10.2

The Eckerd 100 Salute to Women programme

THE ECKERD CORPORATION

The Eckerd Corporation runs a chain of pharmacies and wanted to strengthen its brand identity through the celebration of the 100th anniversary of the opening of its first store. The commercial imperative driving the campaign was the need to stay ahead by building customer loyalty.

Nearly 75% of pharmacy customers are women between 25 and 54. Research showed that this group of women are frequently stressed and turn to trusted sources to reduce stress. Women's trust is based on relationships, and they will be more loyal to a store if they feel an emotional connection to it. The research also showed that there were no emotional connections to women in competitors' messages. From this came the Salute to Women programme, to honour women for their countless hours of helping others.

The campaign aimed to reinforce Eckerd's relevance to its core customers, predominantly women, while positioning the corporation as socially responsible within each community it serves. The programme was also designed to make the public more aware of the corporation within and after its centennial year.

One woman was to be honoured from every Eckerd pharmacy – there are 2,750 outlets in total – and from these, 100 were to be selected as the Eckerd 100. Each woman in the 100 would receive a $1,000 donation to her chosen nonprofit organization, and be invited to a three-day conference on women's issues, called the Eckerd 100 Symposium.

A handbook was devised to lead the 100 district and 2,750 store managers through the Eckerd 100 Search, including point-of-sale display and ballot papers. The launch featured a New York satellite media tour led by the Eckerd President and the US supermodel and community activist, Veronica Webb. Press kits were developed, and template press releases were created to announce results in all the different localities. The symposium was conducted at Emory University's Women's Centre. $1,000 cheques were distributed to the winners, and their own websites were created for them.

CASE STUDY 10.3

Samsung running festival

SAMSUNG ELECTRONICS

Samsung Electronics saw an opportunity to raise its brand awareness and increase sales in the Asian market through its sponsorship of the Bangkok Asian Games. Sponsorship of the Bangkok Asian Games is prestigious but does not automatically bring high brand awareness.

Cheil, the PR consultancy involved, conducted research with 500 consumers and 100 dealers in Thailand, China, and India to establish awareness of the sponsors of the Asian Games as well as brand awareness. Awareness of Samsung as a sponsor was an average 5.6%, while that of its fellow sponsors, Toyota and Acer, was even lower in these three countries, indicating minimal interest in the Games and plenty of room for improvement. Measures of Samsung Electronics' brand awareness were an average of 11.7% unaided and 44.9% when prompted.

The new PR campaign would aim to raise the awareness and sales of Samsung and its products among consumers and dealers in the three target countries, provide practical assistance to athletes competing in the Asian Games and show the commitment of Samsung to the betterment of the local community.

The solution was the development of a running festival which was associated with three key messages: the festival is not a competition but an event open to everybody to raise funds for the athletes; Samsung Electronics sponsors athletes in the games as an official partner; and Samsung is a responsible company that contributes support to the local community.

The Running Festival was held a month before the Games began. Three 5 km 'mini-marathons' started in landmarks in each country, with no entry fee and usage of free promotional T-shirts to attract a crowd. Samsung donated $1 per runner to the relevant sports organizations after the run, totalling $21,000. Coverage in newspapers occurred 136 times, and there were 21 TV reports, as well as a feature programme on STAR TV, which serves an audience of 260 million in 53 countries.

As a result of the PR campaign, the three measures of awareness increased dramatically to 20.4% (sponsorship), 39.1% (unprompted brand awareness) and 64.4% (prompted).

CASE STUDY 10.4

Restoring a national symbol: Topkapi Palace conservation

UNILEVER/CIF

Unilever's Cif household cleaner had a successful promotion in Turkey in 1997 that involved cleaning local monuments. The Cif team came up with the idea of the Cif Cleaning Train which visited cities all over Turkey and achieved a massive media presence as well as an increase in Cif's market share.

Following the success of this, the brand was looking for a similar national campaign to strengthen emotional links between it and the consumer. If a national monument could be selected, and the government agreed, a similar restoration programme could win Cif heightened awareness as the product of a company with respect for the cultures of the society in which its consumers live.

Based on the success of the train campaign, talks were held with the Turkish Minister of Culture, and the Topkapi Palace in Istanbul was identified as being in urgent need of restoration work – the last time it was cleaned and restored was discovered to have been over 500 years ago.

The new PR programme set out to strengthen Cif's brand image and loyalty, and increase brand awareness by increasing the emotional link between consumer and brand. The slogan of the campaign was designed directly to link the brand with the project: 'Let the gleam of the past continue to sparkle in the future.'

The PR plan included the need to communicate that the palace was not being cleaned by Cif products, but only by approved restoration methods. Preliminary project work concluded with the recruitment of an experienced crew, who were to work in Cif uniforms which would ensure the brand appeared in all publicity. A sales campaign and in-store activities were devised, and a complete publicity campaign was created to surround the main event.

An impressive sales conference at the Palace started the project, attended by government representatives. Over the year, all media channels were invited to the restoration work or supplied with continuous restoration news. After the start of work, the Cif TV commercial went on air, and the work reached its climax with the revelation to the media of 300-year-old Ottoman paintings found during the restoration work.

The project received the equivalent of $2.5 million worth of coverage in the media, equal to more than a year of TV advertising. Two million visitors to the palace observed the restoration, and 58% of consumers stated that the campaign strengthened their opinion towards Cif. The brand increased its market share by 3% nationwide.

Defending FedEx's reliability: absolutely, positively, whatever it takes

FEDERAL EXPRESS CORPORATION (FEDEX)

The very foundation of the business of Federal Express Corporation (FedEx) was threatened by a potential pilots' strike in the high volume, pre-holiday season. The strike threat could have driven away customers, upset employee morale, depressed the stock price and alienated the pilots. Avoiding the strike could actually strengthen the business's reputation.

Focus groups organized by the PR team signalled the importance of advance, honest communication about any service problems, particularly among customers who had experienced the previous 1997 UPS strike. Media monitoring several times a day covered messages about FedEx on websites, chat rooms and online newsgroups, permitting responses and fine-tuning of communications content and strategies. Residents of the headquarters' city, Memphis, showed a shift in attitude to the potential strike, in ongoing research following this active management of PR activity.

Ketchum, the PR consultancy, and FedEx conducted twice-daily cross-functional meetings that involved all the departments concerned. The opportunity of enhanced media interest was used to highlight FedEx's strengths in messages that were constantly refined to keep them aligned with company strategy. With customers, this meant stressing the ability to reconfigure the network to remain operational in the event of a strike. With investors, key buy-side and sell-side analysts were contacted to explain the full implications of the FedEx offer and the pilots' union's demands.

A comprehensive campaign to employees used the 'Absolutely, positively, whatever it takes' theme. When the union leadership deprived the pilots of the details of the latest FedEx offer, it was sent directly to pilots' homes. A critical communication from the FedEx founder, Fred Smith, emphasized that the company would not disproportionately compensate any one work group at the expense of others.

In the end, few customers switched their business, and volumes actually increased. Stock rose from $43, when strike ballots went out, to $93 by year-end. The strike was averted, and the first pilot contract with FedEx was ratified by 81% of crew members.

Infantile nutrition, the essence of a generation's health

KRAFT JACOBS SUCHARD

Kraft Jacobs Suchard, a global food manufacturer, initiated a pilot educational programme on infant feeding in Romania, as a contribution to a country with extensive nutritional problems among children.

Due to the lack of financial resources of the Romanian medical system, there is a lack of information on nutrition for children, young mothers and mothers-to-be. A leader in confectionery in Romania since 1995, Kraft Jacobs Suchard saw the opportunity to be associated with bringing real benefits to this community, by filling this information void and adopting a leadership stance in this area.

Data was used from the United Nations Development Programme surveys and national surveys on life quality and nutrition. The results of the analysis showed that a communications programme would be most efficient if addressed to the most vulnerable children and future mothers in the community.

The plan was to develop a pilot educational campaign for the target groups in two cities, for possible national roll-out, in order to influence the public bodies concerned and launch a national debate on the need to educate people on nutrition to bring about a better quality of life.

Kraft Jacobs Suchard consulted representatives from the Ministries of Health and Education, as well as the Institute for Mother and Child Care and the Institute of Nutrition to formulate the messages to be communicated.

The first level of the programme addressed third and fourth grade children, using interactive theatre plays and contests with prizes. The second level addressed the future and young mothers through a brochure entitled 'Healthy Eating Makes Healthy Babies'. Over 1,500 brochures were distributed free of charge to nine medical institutions, and seminars were also organized. Continuous promotion of the events was conducted in the national mass media.

Evaluation was carried out by sending questionnaires to teachers and doctors. The feedback showed that Kraft's project was highly appreciated, and its continuation was requested. The mass-media coverage served to initiate a general debate on the subject. There were 44 press articles, 20 TV items and 17 radio reports on the programme which is to be extended in future years.

CASE STUDY 10.7

State government's $1 billion public offer

AUSTRALIA'S QUEENSLAND GOVERNMENT
TREASURY DEPARTMENT

When Australia's Queensland Government Treasury Department decided to sell its remaining 45% of Suncorp-Metway, a leading financial group, raising over $1 billion, it was the final controversial privatization of a joint bank, building society and rural lender, which was sure to receive political opposition. In addition to managing this issue, the PR team had to explain a complex offer to the public in a way that had to be simple enough to attract Queensland voters, while coping with opposition.

To help to prepare for this campaign and the likely areas of opposition, PR firm, the Phillips Group, conducted an issues review and created a detailed message and audience matrix. A performance analysis of the company was developed, based on broker reports, and extensive stakeholder research was carried out along with in-depth research on political comment going back several years.

The PR campaign set out to support the underwriters in ensuring that the offer was fully subscribed. Specific goals were set around the tone of media coverage that would be needed, that is, that the majority of the coverage should follow the government's agenda and 80% of coverage should contain its key political messages. Another specific objective was that there should be a 50% take-up of the offer by retail investors, mainly in Queensland.

With these goals and issues in mind, key messages were developed, focusing on security, financial return and potential for capital gain. Communication channels were selected – call centres, advertising and direct mail – to communicate the message in a four-week time frame. There was readiness for an earlier cut-off, based on research on public and media reaction.

The offer was positioned as an opportunity for 'mum and dad' investors to participate in the success of Queensland's largest financial institution. The marketing campaign included the offer document, direct mail, advertising, branch promotions and a dedicated call centre. The potential political debate was controlled through a media programme which set the agenda rather than responding to it.

The offer raised $1.012 billion, closed 2.5 times oversubscribed and won more than 60% of investment from 'mum and dad' investors. Over 221,000 applications were received, all of which won an allocation. Out of 138 articles, 128 were positive, and there were 18 positive television reports and 60 radio interviews; 89.6% of stories contained key messages drafted by the Phillips Group and the Treasury. During the offer, no political debate was generated in or out of parliament and the majority of caller feedback included comments on the ease of completing forms.

CASE STUDY 10.8

Post Oreo O's hoop jam contest

OREO COOKIES

The challenge was the launch of a new breakfast cereal into a highly competitive environment. However, the difficult task of launching a new breakfast cereal was helped by associating the *Post* newspaper name with the Oreo brand recognition and equity which is strongly linked to Oreo cookies. The cookies' strongest association is with dunking, and by launching 'slam dunk' contests the brand was able to introduce Post Oreo O's to its target 9–14 age group.

The most popular cookie for kids in the target market was Oreo, and research showed the common interests of boys and girls to be sports, especially basketball, and 'hanging out with friends'. A 'slam and dunk' basketball skills contest would match these interests. It was to be focused on cities with the highest cereal consumption and media opportunities. 'Top 40' (hip-hop, rap and rock) radio programmes were selected to reach the target audience and generate awareness and create a sense of excitement.

The campaign also had to link Oreo O's to the *Post* trademark as well as creating something ownable for Post Oreo O's. The programme also had the clear objective of stimulating the trial of Post Oreo O's. In terms of media coverage targets, this was set to exceed a media impression goal of 38 million.

Once the key messages were defined, different press kits were prepared for both product and events. Background footage was shot for TV, and radio partners were arranged in each market. The cities selected according to the criteria were Minneapolis, Chicago, Dallas and New York, and co-operation with NBA teams was arranged.

The competitions in the four cities had three rounds, and each event was linked to a celebrity local NBA player. Free samples of the new cereal were distributed off-court at each event, and there was full communication to the media.

In the end, the programme generated over 80 million impressions, and every placement contained at least three of the key messages about the cereal's quality and taste. Over 13,000 servings of the cereal were distributed. The target share of the new cereal, set at 0.38%, was reached immediately after the contests were executed, with the year-end share being 0.51%.

CASE STUDY 10.9

Your future is in a forest's past

THE DEPARTMENT OF WOOD TECHNOLOGY,
LJUBLJANA UNIVERSITY, SLOVENIA

The Department of Wood Technology, within the faculty of Biotechnology at Ljubljana University, Slovenia, needed to increase significantly its student and graduate numbers and turned to PR to help.

At less than 50, the number of applicants to join the Department of Wood Technology had been well below the number of places available (70) for a number of years. This was part of a general underrepresentation of the sciences within the university.

The problem was identified through research, which showed that the lack of promotional activity for the department and the fact that it lacked any visual identity in what little literature it produced were major stumbling blocks.

A new PR campaign was devised to inform the target audience of students about the existence and advantages of the study of wood technology. The aim was to increase the number of applicants for the principal vocational degree in the area by 5%, and for the university degree by 10%.

The PR campaign also sought to change attitudes that wood technology was not as prestigious as other studies and to reinforce that this area still offered a prosperous future for graduates. It was also important to position the department as a credible institution that offered a wide array of courses in this field.

A graphic logo for the campaign was devised, based on a human hand symbolizing the future (as in fortune telling) and a tree symbolizing the past. The slogan 'Your future is in a forest's past' was adopted for the communications programme, and leaflets and posters were created. The campaign involved an element which invited school students to take part in a competitive research project on the role of wood in the natural and cultural heritage of their home town.

The promotional material was printed and distributed to 45 Slovenian high schools and seven vocational schools. The new logo was used in all the literature to bring the campaign together. The research project proved to be a great success. Fifty-eight new students applied, far surpassing the organizers' expectations. The mail-out of literature about the course was successful in attracting even more applicants. By the end of the academic period, numbers matriculating for the vocational degree rose by 8.9% and for the university degree by 17.7%.

CASE STUDY 10.10

Just the tablet needed

UNILEVER/PERSIL

Despite being one of the UK's favourite washing powder brands, Lever Brothers was determined to continue to build its market share even further.

The springboard which provided the boost to the brand was the launch of its detergent tablets, which has resulted in Persil regaining market leadership.

When Lever came up with Persil Tablets, seen as the first innovation in the washing powder market for several years, it was the ideal chance to win consumers back and combat speculation about the company's ability to successfully deliver innovative products.

Lever Brothers knew that they needed to create a positive PR environment for the Persil Tablets launch and oversee the product's introduction in key European markets in a co-ordinated and systematic manner in order for the launch to be successful.

While Persil Tablets are a consumer product, Lever felt it was vital that a corporate strategy should be developed, including a risk management strand. The corporate, consumer and public affairs teams consequently worked together on the launch. PR activity began with a programme of pre-briefing of key opinion formers such as UK politicians, particularly those with a Lever factory in their constituencies.

Business journalists and consumer groups with the potential to influence attitudes to both the product and the company were also involved at this stage. To generate confidence in Lever with these groups, the company briefed them with details of the research and testing process which preceded the launch of Persil Tablets, which involved some 100,000 interviews with consumers across Europe.

This was followed by the consumer launch, the core message being that Persil Tablets delivered a measured amount of washing powder, and that, although they may appear expensive on the shelf compared to other products, they offer value for money as there was no wastage and they delivered convenience.

Consumer research identified key consumer targets such as 'bungers' – washing machine-shy young men – and busy mothers, as well as other social groups that would use the new tablets. Targeted news releases were distributed with lifestyle photography to the national and regional media, men's and women's magazines and the lifestyle press, using these social groupings to create relevance and interest.

The company also carefully co-ordinated the roll-out of the launch in Western Europe, developing central guidelines which were distributed to the network of PR agencies handling the launch across the Continent.

The business angle of the launch was well received, and met the campaign's objectives, with stories appearing on the transformation of the Lever business into a fast-moving, innovative market leader. The launch was well covered in the UK by prestigious journals such as the *Financial Times* and on TV by the BBC's *Working Lunch* programme.

The launch was also featured on European consumer programmes including one where a home economist discussed the benefits of the product and said it was good value for money. Other consumer groups across Europe also praised the product for its innovation, convenience and value for money. The launch was also covered widely in the consumer press, from the *Sun* tabloid newspaper to Condé Nast's *Traveller* magazine, *Take a Break* and *FHM*.

Persil's market share has increased since the launch, and the brand has regained its position as the UK's leading washing powder brand. Also, a new Persil Tablet product which cares for coloured fabrics has now been launched.

The launch successfully rebuilt confidence in the company's expertise in new product innovation, a fact that was reflected in Unilever's share price. The amount of research behind the product lent credibility to the launch and interest to the news story.

CASE STUDY 10.11

World Sight Day

LIONS CLUB INTERNATIONAL

Since its inception in 1917, the image of the charity group, the Lions Club International, a group working for the blind, has become diluted, even though 80% of its activities remain sight-related. A new PR campaign built around World Sight Day offered the opportunity for the Lions Club to raise public awareness of the importance of its work and support for blindness prevention campaigns run by governments and nonprofit organizations world-wide.

It was essential that events take place simultaneously in a number of international locations, so extensive cultural research was required to establish partnership opportunities in each of six targeted sites. A suitable date for all locations had to be agreed, and the appropriateness of messages and signage checked for each city chosen.

The aim was to raise public awareness of blindness as a critical heath concern in the world today; to gain support from key governmental and nonprofit organizations; and to seek the participation of Lions' members as part of a bigger campaign showing the organization's commitment to sight preservation.

Thursday 8 October was chosen as the day. A team in Chicago led the international promotion, which also featured in Cape Town, Hong Kong, London, São Paulo and Sydney. Global messages were developed, modified and translated for each venue, in liaison with the local Lions.

Each city had different events, with the collection and recycling of spectacles a common theme, as well as free vision screenings. More than 2,000 people were drawn to the event in São Paulo, and the Lions' commitment to vision was made more evident by the creation of a World Sight Day page on the charity's website.

Around 1.6 billion people were reached through local, national and international media outlets. Over 90% of the items mentioned the Lions and their association with sight preservation. In all, 13 organizations joined the Lions for the day, including the World Health Organization. Thirty thousand spectacles were collected for redistribution in the developing nations and, based on this success, planning for subsequent campaigns is underway.

Lions Clubs International was originally established to 'become knights of the blind in the crusade against darkness'. World Sight Day succeeded in realizing that vision.

CASE STUDY 10.12

Breath Savers
Longest Kiss Challenge

BREATH SAVERS MINTS

This PR programme saw an attention-winning event illustrating the long-lasting effectiveness of Breath Savers mints, and put the Longest Kiss Challenge into world records at the same time.

The association of kissing with the Breath Savers product offered an opportunity to reinforce the brand message 'fresh breath that lasts' in an ambience of fun. The PR team set about finding a kissing-related event that would be suitable for a family audience, as well one that avoided any fears for the safety and hygiene of the participants.

Surveys were conducted with consumers, the media and the Breath Savers sales force to gauge their response to the contest concept. Their fears about possible problems and suggestions for solutions were factored into the ultimate shape and promotion for the kissing contest.

The campaign also had to distinguish Breath Savers from other mints by associating it as the 'kissable mint'. In addition the programme had to deliver the key message that Breath Savers is the mint that delivers fresh breath even after the mint is gone. There was a clear commercial aim to increase sales and the goal was also set to establish a Guinness World Record.

The Longest Kiss Challenge was divided into regional events in 10 cities, during the month of February, with a concentration on Valentine's Day. A strict registration process was devised with a contest time limit of eight hours. The contest was announced over a two-week period with radio spots, accompanied by a regional media plan to ensure that there was active tracking of local contest winners on their way to the finals. On Wednesday March 25, the final event was kicked off live from New York. The contestants were required to remain standing within an area, with lips locked at all times. A Guinness representative judged the contest.

The campaign achieved a 3% increase in sales, and Breath Savers earned an 8% increase in unaided awareness in the breath mint category.

Roberta and Mark Griswold established a world record kiss of 29 hours. World-wide publicity was achieved, with over 400 million impressions in the USA alone.

CASE STUDY 10.13

The history of taste, history of culture and brand awareness

UNILEVER/RAMA MARGARINE

Unilever in Turkey wanted a PR event which could promote their leading margarine brand, Rama, in the Turkish market while being associated with

Unilever's corporate purpose, which is to be a company with 'the highest standards of corporate behaviour towards consumers, societies [and] their cultures'.

The response was to take the 25th anniversary of Rama margarine in Turkey and harness this event to build brand awareness and sales through a successful exhibition of Turkish taste, culture and art.

The company initiated a search for potential artefacts to represent the evolution of taste. The competition was conducted with a committee of history, art and archaeology professors, gourmets and museum directors. Museums and collectors provided the objects, and the theme for the 'Story of taste' was chosen to be 'mother's milk'. A 3,000 BC statue of a breast-feeding woman was chosen as the exhibition's symbol.

The campaign had to strengthen Rama's brand image and increase brand awareness, while linking the concepts of 'preservation of cultural values' and 'taste'. Consequently, the final project slogan was agreed as 'The story of taste started with mother's milk'. The PR company, Green Active, devised supporting advertising, banners, an exhibition catalogue, direct mailings to schools, communications on product labels and in-store activities.

The Ministry of Culture's representative opened the exhibition in Istanbul. Replica exhibition souvenirs were sold, and cakes baked with Rama were served in the Rama Café. During the second week, a 'Hittite night' was organized, offering dishes made from ancient recipes. Early morning school visits were also offered. After 30 days, the 'Story of taste' was moved to Ankara to take part in the 75th anniversary of the Turkish Republic.

In 60 days, 10,000 people in Istanbul and 12,000 people in Ankara visited the exhibition. Media coverage was equivalent to two years of Rama's advertising budget for television, over $2 million in value. After the exhibition, an omnibus survey in Istanbul showed that 76% of consumers stated that their opinion towards Rama was affected positively, 58% stated that the project was very suitable for the brand, and those consumers switching brands to Rama increased by 13%.

Cranium Palladium takes science education centre stage

DOW

From 1988 to 1998, Dow had been running three educational programmes in the USA to fight a continuous decline in national science literacy. Despite this, less than 3% of fourth to twelfth graders reached advanced levels of science education and a new PR programme was devised to renew the attack and revitalize what was an established PR initiative.

The commercial imperative was stark: in 1998, students in the USA were ranked 19th out of 20 industrial nations with regard to science competency. As a major science-based company, Dow needs science skills to be maintained, as fresh, creative thinking was vital to its own commercial progress. PR was seen as a key tool in attracting this top talent to the company.

An analysis of media and academic response to corporate-sponsored graduate recruitment programmes showed that companies were accused of providing propaganda, yet 90% of 229 teachers surveyed on the topic reported that the content of Dow's materials was appropriate for their students' educational level. To build on this, focus groups among students were held which showed a preference for unconventional, interactive and creative learning experiences, with a clear role for those they regarded as peers and role models in any campaign.

The new PR campaign set out to generate positive visibility for Dow and the corporate brand; to reinforce its commitment to innovative science education; and to position Dow as a resource to the education community.

Brainstorming established the name of the programme as Cranium Palladium, which means 'theatre for the mind', and the concept, logo content and script outline were created. Five middle school teachers were recruited to critique the script, and test market performances were launched in three locations. In the test schools, 1,300 students were surveyed and the stylistic elements of the programme were adjusted as a result.

The programme was officially launched and rolled out in 28 large urban high schools, in 25 cities. The PR firm Ketchum prepared media materials and conducted extensive media outreach, heralding the arrival and performances of the Cranium Palladium roadshow in each market. A CD-ROM and interactive video are now being produced to broaden reach into local communities.

The aggregate reach for the programme was 8.3 million, with 94% of all coverage including at least one of three key programme messages. Approximately 46,500 students experienced the live Cranium Palladium production.

CASE STUDY 10.15

Airplane embargo crisis

LAB (BOLIVIAN AIRLINES)

LAB (Bolivian Airlines), the privatized airline, used the following PR campaign to overcome a legal embargo threatening both their business and image, with a programme designed to establish and reinforce their professionalism and innocence in the face of serious allegations.

Opposition to the previously state-owned airline, LAB, followed the 1995 privatization, culminating in an embargo for failure to pay bonuses related to the length of service of employees. The company needed to communicate its responsible attitude and its strengths as an airline, including the very aspect that had prompted the problem – the long experience of its pilots and other employees.

Opinion leaders (politicians, media and travel agencies), customers, businesses and employees were researched extensively prior to the campaign to establish their positions. The main strengths of the company were found to be the professional level of the pilots, the safety record and the price policy. The main weaknesses were found to be poor provision of information to passengers, customer service, fleet obsolescence and communication, both internal and external.

The campaign sought to overcome the legal impasse with the embargo on the airline; minimize damage to the company's image; and recover and recreate a new image. An impact advertising campaign was devised to tackle the embargo, with accelerated courses for the directors in media communication. An audit was conducted, and a plan was devised to implement a communication plan, in which internal communication and staff motivation was recognized as paramount.

The public affairs campaign included meetings with relevant Ministers and the President of the Congress. The media relations plan involved meetings with key editors and journalists and the creation of the LAB media department. The press response system was improved to include tracking and analysis of media coverage and full-scale media training. Usage was made of the LAB internal newsletter to set out the company's case and integrate findings of the new research.

The embargo crisis was resolved with full government recognition that it, rather than the airline's management, was responsible for payment of bonuses for long-time employees. The results of the audit were incorporated into the company's new excellence and quality programme, and the supporting communication plan is now fully in operation as part of the company's standard procedures.

CASE STUDY 10.16

The community benefits from a turnaround at the terminal

THE HAZARDOUS LOAD TERMINAL, PAULINIA

PR played its part in a campaign to encourage oil companies and tanker drivers to use a paid-for, safe terminal for their vehicles at a refinery in Paulinia, Brazil, rather than cause pollution through leaking tankers parked on the public highways. The issue was highlighted by the sight of 1,800 tankers dangerously parked every day for six hours in the town's streets waiting outside the Replan oil refinery, 114 km from São Paulo.

Following a new law which made parking mandatory at every hazardous load terminal (HLT), the new truck parking area at the Paulinia terminal was completed in 1997, with room for 558 tankers, at a cost of $12 million. A centre for truck drivers with a café and other facilities was also built, and the whole complex had a staff of 120.

However, the facility did not prove to be appealing and, as a result, 90 employees were made redundant after the first year.

The PR team identified many errors in launching the 'Paulicentro' terminal, as it was called. These included a lack of pre-announcements or promotional tactics aimed at drivers. Relationships between the centre and the oil distributors were distinctly frosty, and the new centre's name carried very little meaning for potential users of the site, in particular, there was very little linkage with hazard reduction. In addition, those that had used the facility found the complex empty, unfriendly and too costly for meals. They also felt parking there should be free.

In order to rebuild credibility and increase usage by the tanker drivers, a PR campaign was developed to get the terminal accepted and used, at price levels that made it self-financing. The press, natural allies, had to be brought on side, and a new dialogue needed to be established between the centre and the distributors. All these actions needed to take place at the same time to ensure maximum effect.

The name Paulicentro was changed to Hazardous Load Terminal. All the employees were trained in welcoming users, to create a cosier, more friendly environment. Meals at the centre were priced competitively and a press campaign focused on the unique ability of the HLT to receive hazardous vehicles safely, while pointing out the serious environmental effects of oil spills on the water table from vehicles parked on the highway.

Significantly, a deal was made with Shell, which motivated other distributors and brought in a fleet of 450 vehicles. Notices about fines for street parking were posted and fining began.

Within the first month of the campaign, the number of trucks using the HLT had risen to 7,349 over the month. The HLT was completely turned round from an operational viewpoint, and the campaign brought benefits to the community in terms of safety and an improved quality of life.

From a utility to a commercial business

RAILTRACK

This case study shows how Railtrack, a privatized, profit-generating company, avoided a strike, as employees learned to communicate on business objectives and customer relations.

Railtrack plc, the UK's railway infrastructure company, had been focusing on raising performance and the quality of service. The company announced a new investment of £17 billion, and a new focus on internal communications was launched. In the past, internal communications had not been concerned with business issues, but from now on it would be used as a tool to help employees to take on new, profit-related objectives.

The goal of the internal communications programme was to ensure that all staff understood the priority business objectives, and enable them to be clear about their contribution to achieving them. As well as the message delivery, the aim was also to effect a culture change within Railtrack that would develop a habit and process for dialogue between managers and staff about performance, along with new ways of getting information around the organization more accessibly and rapidly.

In approaching internal communications as a key part of the management process, Railtrack's business objectives were identified, together with their relationship with people's day-to-day job performance, attitudes and behaviour. Business operational plans were analysed by the PR team and members of the board were interviewed. Employee attitude surveys were used, and discussions with a broad range of managers were conducted.

Critical success factors were identified, the most challenging being that internal communication should be seen as being as important as external. The concept of 'rights' and 'responsibilities' about information was developed, to change the way that internal communication was viewed, talked about and used inside the business. It was to be unacceptable for employees to be kept in the dark or claim they didn't need to know.

New targets were set that stipulated that all information should reach all (previously 65%) employees within 24 hours. The staff were to have the opportunity to meet senior management, achieved by a series of 'railshows'. Knowledge sharing on best practice was achieved by the creation of new internal media. 'Teamtalk' and other innovative new programmes were introduced.

The speed of communication achieved was pivotal in avoiding strike action that would have affected the rail companies. Post-event research also showed that over 90% of the staff who attended the railshows felt that they could link their objectives to those of their zone and the company overall.

CASE STUDY 10.18

The incontinence project

PHARMACIA UPJOHN

More than five million Germans suffer from urinary incontinence, but it is such a taboo subject that over 45% of those afflicted do not mention the problem even to their doctor. There is very little media reporting on it and limited public knowledge of its causes or the various brands available for its treatment, including Detrusitol, manufactured by Pharmacia Upjohn.

The first step in the company's PR campaign was to carry out surveys among doctors, nurses and pharmacists on the subject of self-medication for incontinence. The company also organized discussions with self-help groups and experts. It was found that medical treatment and help is essential in tackling all facets of the problem, therefore their support in the PR campaign was going to be vital.

The PR sought to inform the public and patients about the problem and encourage sufferers to consult their doctors. 'Discuss the problem with your doctor and don't suffer in isolation' was the simple key message. Another strand of the PR looked to heighten doctors' awareness of the subject and inform them about the brands used in the treatment of this condition, including Detrusitol.

An information tour was planned, in conjunction with the leading self-help society for incontinence sufferers and the health-related magazine *Frau im Spiegel*. Releases were written and the itinerary was designed to achieve maximum media coverage. A nation-wide information tour visited 24 towns and cities over a six-week period. Advanced coverage, appearances by medical anchor men from regional medical TV programmes, debates, leaflets, one-on-one meetings between doctors and sufferers and an interactive hotline were all featured at local level. There was strong support from the national media which responded well to the total media package on offer from the company.

As a result of the information tour, 33,000 direct contacts were made with the public, 42 million media impressions were achieved with a high percentage requesting further information. A further 31 million media impressions were generated through media partnerships. The tour stimulated 316 articles in the media with a total circulation of 73.1 million. The frequency of editorial reports on this subject almost tripled compared to the previous year.

Against a background of the legal prohibition of the advertising of ethical drugs, the company succeeded in using PR to communicate to its target audience about an embarrassing and difficult subject.

CASE STUDY 10.19

'Let's stop the silent killer'

HUNGARIAN NATIONAL HEALTH PROTECTION INSTITUTE

Hungary has a major problem with hypertension, caused by unhealthy lifestyles involving tobacco, alcohol and fat-rich food. This is exacerbated by low budgets for health education to increase public awareness of the issues involved.

The high mortality from heart disease in Hungary, caused by high blood pressure, has been unaffected by government warnings, which to date had lacked strength and efficacy. So a new campaign, run by the Hungarian National Health Protection Institute (NEVI), part of the Ministry of Public Welfare, sought to partner with the private sector in order to deliver a more powerful campaign that drew on the strength, expertise and funds of the private sector.

Media analysis and research showed that information about hypertension typically concentrated on frightening the public by constant repetition of the negative effects of related diseases. As many as 70% of interviewees stated that this was ineffective and boring, turning them away from interesting material about medical advances and understanding of the issue.

The task was therefore to define a new, more engaging message about hypertension; to create a new channel to deliver it through ; and to find a style that would be interesting, relevant and which reached a large public.

A 'health show' was chosen as the medium, linked with the traditional May Day celebration in the capital. A gigantic tent was erected in the city park, free blood pressure tests and medical advice were on offer and the slogan 'Take it to heart' was devised as the platform for the event and the surrounding publicity campaign.

Invitations were sent to leading journalists to attend the results of an international study in Amsterdam. It aimed to introduce them to the Netherlands' practices in the prevention, treatment and aftercare of hypertension, and encourage informed and entertaining media coverage. The pre-campaign research had shown that this was the most likely route to attracting public attention, rather than the more traditional 'stern warnings' about healthy lifestyles. A high profile blood pressure measurement of MPs was also negotiated to add further popular appeal to the campaign.

Almost 13,000 people attended the 'Take it to heart' public health show, and 3,500 people had their blood pressure taken, including over 500 acute cases. The associated media campaign reached 70% of the Hungarian population, assisted by the feedback from the visit to Amsterdam and the taking of MPs' blood pressure.

The resultant PR campaign successfully reached the public in Budapest with support from the Astra Pharmaceuticals Company – the health authorities' private sector partner for the campaign. Consequently, the number of people requesting measurement of their blood pressure has increased significantly in the capital city and as a result of the success of this initiative, a new campaign will now target the whole of Hungary.

Negotiations for a collective agreement

HEALTH CARE UNION OF SLOVENIA (HUS)

HUS, the union for nurses and healthcare technicians in Slovenia, had traditionally not been strong enough to persuade the government to sit with it to negotiate a collective agreement on rates of pay and working conditions. The union aims to achieve better working conditions for its members and a higher level of appreciation of its members' work. A collective agreement with the government would achieve most of its targets, if it could persuade the government to work more closely with its officials.

Another issue was that membership of HUS did not represent all the relevant skills within the industry, and the union had members who were unmotivated and disorganized. In addition, the union was unknown to the media. To turn this position around, a communications campaign was developed with the aim of negotiating a collective agreement with the government.

Underpinning this, there would need to be a new effort to improve communication between members and union officials. Better links with media had to be established and a recruitment drive for new members was launched as part of the campaign in order to increase the number, status and negotiating power of nurses and technicians within HUS.

The first campaign with the media and opinion formers set out the case for improved conditions for nurses, generating 840 articles in the press in one year, an extraordinary achievement in a mass media that had previously ignored the existence of HUS. The number of union members rose from 6,000 to 7,500. The union's president, Mrs Jelka Cemlvec, was nominated as one of the candidates for the Slovenian Woman of the Year award. The government responded to pressure, and renewed negotiations took place from a far stronger position.

Communication against child sex tourism

The number of children in developing countries forced into prostitution has grown to over two million world-wide. Many of their abusers are from the West. At the start of the 1990s, laws were passed in some European Union countries making the sexual abuse of children abroad a crime that can be prosecuted in the perpetrator's native country.

The fight against child sex tourism required public warnings to prospective abusers, such as long-distance travellers, but it also needed to reach all travellers, in order to raise awareness of this issue. Therefore, a forceful and sensitive PR campaign was devised by the authorities to reach both target audiences.

Pre-campaign research showed that it would be best to approach travellers directly on the aircraft, using the in-flight video programme. But airlines had to be convinced that they could cope with issues that might arise. As a result, the key action was identified as winning the airlines' agreement, aided by press and PR work.

Research with experts in communications and tourism in 13 European countries established the criteria for developing the in-flight video. The research made it plain that to be effective the video must be capable of use internationally; the content should be understandable without a headset if seen on a plane; it should be suitable for family viewing; and it should not have a duration of more than 60 seconds.

The video was to be the central plank of the campaign, and was designed to prevent child sex tourism by confronting travellers and airline employees with the issues raised. The aim was to sensitize and encourage them to talk to perpetrators and potential perpetrators, in order to directly discourage them rather than looking the other way. Part of this message was a clear warning that this is a crime punishable at home.

Treatments for the video were created and selected with the help of international experts. Lufthansa, Germany's national airline carrier, was recruited as an initial partner in order to encourage other European airlines to participate. The video was shown to them, first as a storyboard and then in its final form.

Post-campaign evaluation recorded the media support work resulted in 30 million contacts. Of those surveyed in a post-campaign poll, 89% agreed that the video was suitable for sensitizing travellers, and 52% said that it directly challenged viewers to help to address the issues raised.

CASE STUDY 10.22

Educational television

ABS/CBN FOUNDATION

Sixty per cent of the population of the Philippines live in poverty, and there are ill-equipped schools with a student to teacher ratio of 75:1. The ABS/CBN broadcasting network set up the Foundation to win the social involvement of the public and private sectors in making effective educational TV programmes (ETV) available to every school.

Besides the low competence of students, research showed that only 2 out of 10 children wanted to be Filipino. Both motivation and educational opportunity are needed for a better self-image, based on educational excellence.

The campaign set out to change this by developing a generation of value-oriented and globally competitive students with a strong sense of nationalism and cultural pride. This was to be achieved by making ETV accessible to 100% of the public elementary school population by the year 2004.

The programmes each involved the synergy and collective efforts of national experts and institutions. The company's logistics and operations department was tasked to find financial support for ETV, with the goal of installing a monitor in every school. The number of advertisers on the programme has been grown to reach a current total of 16. Videos and parent–teacher manuals were created, and conventions were organized for principals and school administrators.

The number of programmes was extended from the previous three science and heritage modules, to include mathematics and an English course. A total of 4,662 cable-ready TV monitors have now been donated. The programmes were in the top five most watched children's programmes in the country.

The ETV programmes won five international prizes for the quality of their programmes in 1998. Beyond any role as part of the public relations of ABS/CBN, it is established as a long-term public service benefiting the entire Philippine nation and society. ETV in the Philippines has brought extended learning opportunities to 14 million students, at no charge, in a country ranked among the lowest in the world for science and mathematics competence.

CASE STUDY 10.23

Working with charities

UNILEVER/PERSIL

The Persil detergent brand was looking to create PR support for the brand's sponsorship of the charity, Comic Relief, in 1999, which was estimated to raise £250,000 from the sale of special packs.

The company set itself the task of building awareness of Persil Colour Care through the sponsorship of Red Nose Day, a special fund-raising day organized by UK charity Comic Relief, while communicating the key brand message that 'Persil Colour Care takes care of and keeps your colours bright'. In addition, Unilever required the brand to be championed as the main sponsor of the event, since over 10 other companies were supporting the charity.

The company created the concept 'Go Red for Comic Relief and Stay Red with Persil Colour Care' as a natural link for the brand to communicate key messages in a fun way. This involved using a variety of media including radio, consumer magazines with a number of mechanics, such as competitions, offers and promotions as well as editorial negotiation to encourage the UK to 'Go Red' by taking on a red theme for the day.

All activity culminated in the cheque presentation on Red Nose Day, shown on BBC TV (viewership 3 million) on 12 March 1999, which involved six hunky men wearing Persil branded T-shirts stripping to their Persil-white boxer shorts to the tune of 'Heard it through the grapevine' to reveal the grand total of money raised by Persil printed on their shorts!

The brand succeeded in creating a sense that the nation was 'Going Red' by providing both journalists and the general public with easy-to-use mechanics for fund-raising activity, in addition to maintaining the key Persil Colour Care product messages in the majority of communications.

CASE STUDY 10.24

Taking the high ground in the hygiene debate

UNILEVER/DOMESTOS

Domestos is a major brand of household bleach and related cleaning products sold throughout the world under a variety of brand names. In Europe, the brand wanted to differentiate itself by developing a leadership position as 'The hygiene expert', in particular to mothers with children under 10 years.

PR was seen to be the ideal educational tool to inform these consumers about hygiene issues, providing practical help and advice in an area where considerable ignorance and confusion still exists.

Unilever, the brand owner, set about developing a PR strategy that would establish the Domestos brand as *the* hygiene experts across Europe, using an approach that married the emotional and rational responses to hygiene issues.

It took the form of a key stage programme that, when rolled out, would generate widespread awareness of hygiene issues within the family and position Domestos as *the* hygiene experts offering practical help and advice.

The foundation for the key stage programme was the creation and development of a branded 'advisory service' in each country. Each advisory service had an identity, a contact point, such as a phone-in/written careline, consumer literature on all aspects of hygiene including food, home and baby hygiene and, above all, independent spokespersons, all experts in the field of hygiene, who would speak for and on behalf of the brand.

The role of the first of the four key stages was to gain credibility and awareness for the advisory service among health professionals, such as health visitors and community nurses, all identified as primary opinion formers among the target audience of mothers with young children.

Once this level had been achieved and maintained, the Advisory Service would proactively seek to engage new and first-time mothers, both directly through mother and baby shows or specific sponsorship initiatives as well as via a targeted media relations programme. As each markets' programmes evolved, key stages 3 and 4 began employing tactics that interacted with the consumer at nonmedia levels too, such as roadshows, exhibitions and ultimately, a dedicated 'hygiene awareness week'.

The public awareness campaign is now in its fourth year with all major Uniever markets having now developed activity up to key stage 4. It is significant that all markets continue to support the base platform of promoting good hygiene practice to health professionals, maintaining a contact programme through seminars, newsletters and making available branded literature.

CASE STUDY 10.25

The maiden cruise crisis that turned itself around

P&O CRUISES

The maiden voyage on 1 May 2000 of P&O Cruises' newest superliner, the £200 million *Aurora*, was prefaced by two weeks of concentrated promotional activity, the climax to an ongoing programme lasting almost three years to introduce her to the consumer and travel industry via the media.

PR-led initiatives around important milestones in *Aurora*'s evolution were designed to address the core communications objectives and complement the ship's dedicated advertising campaign. Activity achieved target outputs agreed with the client, making *Aurora* very high profile on departure.

The day after *Aurora*'s send-off from Southampton, P&O Cruises' public relations teams world-wide were alerted to the fact that something had gone wrong on the ship. Immediately, a crisis team was convened to oversee the communications management of this high profile project.

After less than 16 hours and 300 miles of the voyage, *Aurora* had suffered a technical problem (an overheating propeller shaft bearing), necessitating abrupt termination of the cruise. At risk was irreparable damage to the reputation of the ship and that of P&O Cruises.

The PR team was tasked with objectives based on the protection of P&O Cruises' reputation as the UK's leading cruise operator. The team knew it had to work to ensure that negative publicity was minimized by giving the media factually accurate information, thus reducing the risk of erroneous speculation. Another key objective was to reassure passengers booked on subsequent cruises that there would be no impact on their holiday plans.

P&O Cruises operated a crisis management strategy which sought to:

- advise the media that *Aurora* was returning to port

- make P&O Cruises managing director, Gwyn Hughes, supported by other senior management, accessible for broadcast media interviews

- be open and frank about the problem and sympathize with the enormous disappointment being felt by the 1,600 plus maiden cruise passengers

- hold a clarifying news conference at Southampton soon after docking on 3 May with Gwyn Hughes and Captain Steve Burgoine

- give media access to disembarking passengers to avoid any impression that there was anything to hide.

So when, at 10.30 on 2 May, a public address by the captain advised passengers that *Aurora* was returning to Southampton in the UK, long-standing crisis communications contingency plans were immediately put into place.

P&O Cruises proactively announced details of *Aurora*'s difficulty to media. The first statement was drafted, approved and had begun to be issued within one hour of the initial briefing. For the next 48 hours, the inhouse PR team played a pivotal role in the communications process with the media and as the co-ordinator for broadcast media interview requests.

Key media were called/emailed/faxed with the statement, consolidating trusting relationships that had been developed over years of handling PR for P&O Cruises. By 19.00 on day one some 110 media calls had been addressed by the team. It was also recommended that P&O hold a press conference in Southampton soon after *Aurora*'s return to port (3 May) and before passengers disembarked. Some 45 media persons attended. Further updated bulletins were issued when *Aurora* left Hamburg in Germany on 13 May after repairs and a news conference was held with Captain Burgoine at Southampton before the ship resumed her cruise programme, on schedule, on 15 May.

The media interest throughout was intense: broadcast media (38 TV and 131 radio bulletins), national (38) and regional (233), newspapers, specialist and shipping press (58) and Internet bulletin boards all gave extensive coverage to *Aurora*'s problems between 1 and 16 May.

Inevitably, the words 'breakdown' and 'embarrassment' figured in the more emotive reporting. But, overwhelmingly, the coverage was sympathetic, due primarily to a rapid admission of the problem and the company's willingness to discuss it frankly and honestly.

The generous compensation package for passengers figured prominently in coverage. Because it acted swiftly with suitable financial redress, P&O Cruises emerged as a trusted and caring holiday provider, committed to customer satisfaction and therefore bucking the trend in the media's eyes.

Throughout events, the media frequently took the opportunity to reiterate how *Aurora* had advanced cruise ship design with its range of luxury facilities, thus adding to the ship's lustre. P&O Cruises' Chairman Lord Sterling commended the PR team for a 'crisis well handled'.

If it was not before, *Aurora* is now arguably one of the world's best-known cruise ships. And the fact that there was not a single cancellation and that berths on the ship were more than 90% sold for the remainder of the 2000 cruise programme is testimony that *Aurora* emerged unscathed from the crisis.

Recommended further reading

Armstrong, M. *Human Resource Management* (Kogan Page, 1998).

Bernstein, D. *Company Image and Reality* (Cassell, 1991).

Cannon, T. *Corporate Responsibility* (Pitman, 1994).

Ceserani, J. and Greatwood, P. *Innovation and Creativity* (Kogan Page, 1996).

Curtin, T. with Jones, J. *Managing Green Issues* (Macmillan – now Palgrave, 2000).

Dauphinais, W. and Price, C. *Straight from the CEO* (Nicholas Brealey, 1999).

Dixit, A.K. and Nalebuff, B.J. *Thinking Strategically* (WW Norton, 1993).

Guillery, J.-M. and Ogrizek, M. *Communicating in Crisis* (Walter de Gruyter, 1999).

Hamel, G. *Leading the Revolution* (Harvard Business School Press, 2000).

Klein, N. *No Logo* (Flamingo, 2001).

Knasel, E., Meed, J. and Rossetti, A. *Learn for your Life* (Pearson Education, 2000).

Knobil, M. *Superbrands* (Creative and Commercial Communications, 1998).

McDonald, M. and de Chernatony, L. *Creating Powerful Brands* (Butterworth Heinemann, 2000).

Mallinson, B. *Public Lies and Private Truths* (Cassell, 1996).

Olins, W. *The New Guide to Identity* (Gower, 1999).

Pine II, B.J. and Gilmore, J.H. *The Experience Economy* (Harvard Business School Press, 1999).

Ridderstrale, J. and Nordstrom, K. *Funky Business* (Pearson Education, 2000).

Schultz, M., Hatch, M.J. and Larsen, M.H. *The Expressive Organisation* (Oxford University Press, 2000).

Smythe, J., Dorward, C. and Reback, J. *Corporate Reputation* (Century Business, 1992).

Spillane, M. *Branding Yourself* (Pan Books, 2000).

Stone, N. *The Management and Practice of Public Relations* (Macmillan – now Palgrave, 1995).

Wheeler, D. and Sillanpaa, M. *The Stakeholder Corporation* (Pitman, 1997).

Index

Entries in this index are arranged in alphabetical order, letter-by-letter. **Bold** type indicates principal entries.

ABS/CBN, 82, 186–7
Allen, Woody, 64
arts PR, *see* PR campaigns
Ashdown, Sir Paddy, 26
Astra Pharmaceuticals, 183
Atherton, Mike, 26
audiences, *see* stakeholders
Aurora, *see* P&O Cruises

Bell, Martin, 25
Bellamy, David, 27
Bellingham, Lynda, 26
Bhopal, 8
Bird, Dickie, 26
Blackman, Honor, 27
Blethyn, Brenda, 25
Body Shop, The, 22, 48
Boeing, 47
Bolivian Airlines, 76, 177–8
Bracken, Kyran, 25
Breath savers mints, 173–4
BSE, 35
Burson-Marsteller, 45

Career development, 13–14, 98–9
Cato, Roger, 26
Catt, Mike, 24
cause-related marketing, 48, 187
CBN, *see* ABS/CBN
CEO, role of, *see* spokespeople, importance of
charity related PR, *see* PR campaigns
Cheil Communications, 162
child sex tourism, 185
Churchill, Winston, 91, 106, 144
Cleese, John, 25
Coca Cola, 47–9
    Sprite Ball, 14, 23–4
Collins, Phil, 25
communications audit, 71

Communications Group, the, 160
consultancy, PR
    gaining value from, 116–17, 120–1, **122–5**, 127
    growth of, 8, 113–16
    gurus, qualities of, 125–6
    relationships with clients, 123–5
    selection of, 121–2
    when to use, 118–20
consumer PR, *see* PR campaigns
consumerism, rise of, 5–7, 40–4, 45–6
corporate PR, *see* reputation management
corporate social responsibility, 7, 48–9
creativity, 82–3, 86
crisis management, 8–9, 48, **70–3**, 75, 165, 177–8, 189–91
    see also the Internet – crisis and issues management

Davies, Alan, 26
Dawn, Elizabeth, 26
Dell, Michael, 87
De Vito, Danny, 107
Dimbleby, Jonathan, 27
Dow, 176–7
drivers, of reputation, *see* evaluation
Dunkin' Donuts, 143

Eckard 82–3, 161–2
E. coli, 35
educational PR, *see* PR campaigns
e-economy, *see* the Internet
employee communications, *see* internal communications
evaluation, of reputation management and PR, 83–4
    drivers, of reputation, 58–61
    reputation scorecard, 61, 63
    reputation score/index, 62–3, 65
    see also Fortune; Financial Times, Management Today

Federal Express, 76, 165
Financial Times, 57–9
Fombrun, Charles, 58–9
Fortune, 57–9

Gap, 38
Gates, Bill, *see* Microsoft
General Electric, *see* Welch, Jack
genetically modified organisms, *see* Monsanto
genome, the PR, 52–3
Gerrard, Paul, 28
Gestetner, 82–3, 160–1
globalization, 38, **47–8**

Health Canada, 22
healthcare PR, *see* PR campaigns
hemp, promotion of, 22
Hendry, Stephen, 24
Hesmondalgh, Julie, 26
Hungarian Health Authority, 97
Hungarian National Health Protection Institute, 182–3

IKEA, 143
internal communications, 148
    cascade briefings, 154–6, 157–9
    HR, to support, 151–2
    Intranets, 138–9
    leaflets, 154
    mission statements, 155–6
    motivational, 150–1
    newsletters, 154
    planning for, 153, 156–7
    videos, 154
Internet, the
    anti-sites, 143
    chat rooms, 145
    consumer dialogue on, 131–2, 134–6
    crisis and issues management, 141–5
    impact on reputation, 128–30
    internal communications, 138–9
    Intranets, 138
    myths of, 130

Index

online journalists, 132–4,
online monitoring, 142
opinion formers, 139
websites, 134–6, 137–8,
139–40, 146–7,
investment, attraction of, 15
issues management, 17–18,
70–3, *see also* the Internet –
crisis and issues management

Janis, Peter, 25
Johnson, Luke, 25
joined up reputation
management, 76–80

Kane, Andy, 27
Kennedy, John F, 91
Ketchum Communications, 165
King, Oona, 26
Kraft Jacobs Suchard, 69,
166–7

Levi Strauss, 141
Lineker, Gary, 27
Lions Club International, 172–3
Ljubljana University, 100, 169
Lufthansa, 185
Lulu, 28
Lumley, Joanna, 25

Management Today, 57–9
Maslow, hierarchy of needs, xi
McCann Erickson, 20
McDonald's, 38, 47, 143–4
measurement, *see* evaluation
media
    fragmentation of, 4–5, 46–7
    speed of, 6
    see also the Internet –
    online journalists
media training, 73–5
mergers and acquisitions, 15
messages
    development of, 90, 94
    facts to support, 92–3, 96–7
    mapping, **92–5,** 106
    master messages, 90
    trident, 91, 93
Microsoft, 49, 87
Mirran, Helen, 27
monitoring, 81–2, *see also* the
    Internet – online monitoring
Monsanto, 35–6
Moore, Peter, 25
MORI, 61–2

New York University, *see*
    Fombrun, Charles
Nike, 8, 23, 38
Nikon, 47, 141.

Oreo, *see* Post Oreo O

P&O Cruises, 48, 189–91
Paulicentro Hazardous Load
    Terminal, 72, 178–9
personal reputation
    development, **19–21,** 24–8
Pharmacia Upjohn, 97, 181–2
Phillips Group, the, 167–8
Post Oreo O, 82, 168–9
PR campaigns
    arts, 160
    charity related, 172, 187–8
    consumer, 163, 168–9,
        170–2, 173–5, 188–9
    educational, 176–7, 185–7
    healthcare, 161, 166–7,
        181–3
    planning of, 99–100
    public sector, 167–8,
        169–7, 184
    sports, 162
    technology, 160
presentation skills, 104–5,
    106–8
    dramatic gestures, 111–12
    master messages, 90
    physical appearance, 109–10
    props, 108
    soundbites, 105
    to staff, 157–9
pro bono work, 98–9
public sector PR, *see* PR
    campaigns

Queensland Treasury
    Department, 90, 167–8
question and answer
    documents, 73

Railtrack, 148, **156–7**
regulatory support
    influencing legislation,
        16–17
    planning permission, 16
reputation consultative group,
    57–61, 64
reputation drivers, *see*
    evaluation
reputation flow, 77
reputation ladder, 68
reputation management
    building of, 51–2, **78**
    importance of, 1–3
    planning of, 29, **31–50,**
        54–7, 80, 100–3, 153,
    rise of, **3–9,** 30, 49, 51
    see also internal
        communications, planning
risk management, *see* crisis
    management
Robson, Bryan, 26

Roddick, Anita, 22
Romanian Health Authority,
    69, 166–7

Sales support, 14, 17
Samsung, 82, 162–3
Shakespeare, William, 105
Sharman, Helen, 27
Shell, **8–9,** 38
    anti-site, 143
    Brent Spar, 8
    Nigeria, 9
Slovenia, Healthcare Union of,
    184–5
Sony, 47
Spacey, Kevin, 107
spokespeople
    development of, 89
    importance of, 86–9, 124,
        158–9
    see also presentation skills
sports PR, *see* PR campaigns
staff, recruitment and
    retention, 15
stakeholders
    convergence of, 31, **45**
    opinion formers, 3–5, 37–8,
        66–9
    see also Internet – opinion
        formers
Stern Business School, *see*
    Fombrun, Charles
Strategic Objectives Inc., 22
supplier relationships, 16
Syal, Meera, 27

Target audiences, *see*
    stakeholders
technology PR, 160, *see* PR
    campaigns, *see also* the
    Internet
Tesco, 141
Toyota, 36
trident messages, *see* messages
Turkey, *see* Unilever, Cif;
    Unilever, Rama

Unilever
    Cif, 69, 82, 163–4
    Domestos, 14, 188–9
    Persil, 34, 48, 170–2, 187–8
    Rama, 83, 174–5
United Nations
    Anan, Kofi, 28
    Food and Agricultural
        Organisation, 35

Weber Shandwick, 38, 58,
Welch, Jack, 87
Wilde, Oscar, xi, 106
Wolstenholme, Kenneth, 27